SCHOOL CURRICULUM
ISSUES AND CONCERNS

Books by **Marlow Ediger**
and
Digumarti Bhaskara Rao

Administration of Schools
Community Colleges
Curriculum Organisation
Curriculum of School Subjects
Effective Schooling
Effective School Curriculum
Elementary Curriculum
Elementary Curriculum Improvement
Essays on Teaching Mathematics
Essays on Teaching Science
Essays on Teaching Social Studies
Essays on Teaching Reading
Essays on Teaching and Learning
Improving School Administration
Issues in School Curriculum
Language Arts Curriculum
Philosophy and Curriculum
Psychology and Curriculum
Quality School Education
Reading Curriculum and Instruction
Relevancy in Elementary Curriculum
School Organisation
School Curriculum and Administration
Science Curriculum
Teaching English Successfully
Teaching Language Arts Successfully
Teaching Mathematics Successfully
Teaching Science Successfully
Teaching Social Studies Successfully
Teaching Mathematics in Elementary Schools
Teaching Science in Elementary Schools
Successful School Administration
Successful School Education

published by
Discovery Publishing House Pvt. Ltd.

SCHOOL CURRICULUM
ISSUES AND CONCERNS

By

Prof. Marlow Ediger

B.S.E., M.A., Ed.D. (Education)
Emeritus Professor of Education
Truman State University
201 West 22nd Street
North Newton KS 67117
United States of America
mediger2@cox.net

&

Prof. Digumarti Bhaskara Rao

M.Sc., M.A., M.A., M.Ed., Ph.D.
Dean, Faculty of Education
Member, Academic Senate
Ex-Chairman, Board of Studies in Education
Member, Research Advisory Committee
Acharya Nagarjuna University
D-43, S.V.N. Colony
Guntur - 522 006 (India)
digumartibhaskararao@rediffmail.com

DPH

DISCOVERY PUBLISHING HOUSE PVT. LTD.
NEW DELHI-110 002

Published by:
Tilak Wasan
DISCOVERY PUBLISHING HOUSE PVT. LTD.
4383/4B, Ansari Road, Darya Ganj
New Delhi-110 002 (India)
Phone : +91-11-23279245, 43596064-65
Fax : +91-11-23253475
E-mail : discoverypublishinghouse@gmail.com
sales@discoverypublishinggroup.com
web : www.discoverypublishinggroup.com

First Edition: **2015**

ISBN: 978-93-5056-723-4

School Curriculum: *Issues and Concerns*

Printed at:
Infinity Imaging Systems
Delhi

Dedicated
to

Digumarthi Family

PREFACE

School curriculum is the planned interaction of students with instructional content, materials, resources, and processes for evaluating the attainment of educational objectives. It is prescriptive and is based on a more general syllabus which specifies what topics must be understood and to what level to achieve a particular standard. It refers to all courses offered at a school. It also refers to a defined and prescribed course of studies, which students must fulfil in order to pass a certain level of education. Its transaction takes place by the use of literacies and datagogies that are interwoven through the use of digital media and/or texts/books that address the complexities of teaching and learning.

Many issues and concerns concerned to school curriculum are discussed in detail in this book. This book will be of great use to the curriculum specialists, textbook writers, teachers and administrators at school stages.

Digumarti Bhaskara Rao

CONTENTS

1

School Curriculum

(Issues and Concerns)

There are selected issues which face schools in curriculum development. These need thorough study by those involved and are affected by decisions made. There are a plethora of outside forces as well as those that are involved within the school setting which affect outcomes of choices studied and implemented. School personnel must become students of education and of the curriculum (Ediger and Rao, 2012).

Which Issues are Current?

Spending for public schools by each state has been greatly curtailed. The reduced spending has caught up with the lower state aid available to the local school district. Teachers have been laid off and more will be terminated with new spending cuts in the offing. Adequate amounts of moneys must be spent on teacher salaries, materials of instruction, educational technology, textbooks and library books, inservice training, among other necessities. Today's children will be the adult citizens of the future. Each pupil needs an education which will bring out the best in the individual and provide for optimal progress. The question arises, "How might an increased amount of money be secured for the public schools. State legislatures cut appropriations in order to reduce taxing people. The argument here, given by the governor and the state legislature, is that lower income tax brings in more businesses into the local state. The flip side of this argument are the following:

- business establishments also desire high quality schools for their offspring.

- pupils need to realize optimal school achievement in order to do well in a complex world.

Second, mandated testing has been weighed and found wanting. The No Child Left Behind law of 2002 whereby each state in the nation developed their own criteria for tests found there was great variation on the complexity of test items among these tests. Now, the emphasis is upon the Common Core State Standards adopted by for forty six states. The tests for each grade level will be the same, thus avoiding the difficulty levels of test items among and between the states. More uniformity will be in evidence when comparing pupil achievement from state to state. However individual differences among pupils will exist in the following:

- the rapidity in responding to the test; some need more time than others in test taking.
- learning styles of pupils in taking pencil/paper testing as compared to a hands on approach in revealing what has been accomplished.
- thinking and creativity are minimized by pupils when taking objective test items, such as multiple choice.

Third, bullying in schools has truly been a problem which needs identification and solutions in each school. Bullying makes for fear of perpetrators and hinders achievement greatly. Then too, it is not good for perpetrators to get by with offending others. This hinders their development socially and emotionally. Each case of reported bullying needs to be looked into carefully and recorded with remedies in the offing.

Fourth, physiological needs of pupils must be met in school. Thus, breakfast and dinner need to be served and available to all pupils. This still leaves a weakness with one omitted meal in the evening. Sending home a package of food, adequate for the week end is a must. This should be the right of every child along with living in a clean, safe and home environment.

Fifth, medical care, too frequently, is lacking for pupils. Learners cannot achieve well if salient unmet health care is there. There are medical needs which should be available for all pupils. Governmental help is definitely needed. Those who argue for a smaller government would generally like to see social services cut in order to have more "money in the pockets" of individuals, as a cost cutter. These are cases involving morality and empathy when helping people in need (Ediger, 2009).

Sixth, the curriculum must be updated with the latest innovations in assisting learners to do better in school and in society. This is costly, yes, but more so if a modern curriculum does not exist. For example, electronic readers would help many pupils to learn to read better than otherwise is the case. Thus, a pupil can go ahead in dependently with an electronic reader which provides assistance as necessary in vocabulary and reading difficulties. The electronic reader then may provide oral content in which the learner may follow along with the pronounced words in print. Vocabulary terms, unknown, may be highlighted and the appropriate definition seen on the monitor. Independently, he/she may move forward in subject matter read. This would do away with problems, to a large extent, in word recognition and make for more fluent reading. Innovations need to be tried out to notice if pupils do achieve more optimally. Education costs money, but is more costly if pupils leave school without the tools of being successful in reading and the language arts, science, social studies, the fine arts, and physical education. Physical education, as a quality course, is indeed necessary to curb obesity.

Seventh, thinking must be emphasized in each curriculum area. The concept of thinking may be divided into component parts but needs to be integrated into ongoing lessons/units of study:

- critical thinking involves analyzing ideas into facts versus opinion, accurate from the inaccurate, as well as the relevant from the irrelevant.

- creative thought whereby novel, unique and originality is stressed.

Eighth, integration of subject matter from the different academic disciplines is to be emphasized if this aids pupils in establishing meaning and understanding. Otherwise, there is appropriateness in maintaining clarity between and among these disciplines. Thus, in a unit of study, the teacher must be savvy in knowing how much integration in relating the diverse disciplines is to be emphasized. In many situations, it is good to have learners perceive the relationship of concepts and generalizations which cut across the diverse subject matter areas. Too frequently, each lesson/unit of study has stressed isolated facts with little/no attempts at uniting ideas and thoughts from the academics. Isolated subject matter is more difficult to retain and recall as compared to that which joins together whereby pupils may connect the previously acquired concepts and generalizations with the ensuing content to be achieved.

Ninth, valid and reliable appraisal techniques need to be utilized to aid the teacher in understanding what learners have accomplished. For the classroom teacher, face validity is very appropriate to utilize. Here, the teacher writes a test item for each major concept/generalization taught. The test item may be multiple choice with four equivalent distractors or an essay test. Oral testing might also be stressed in that questions are asked and responses given by learners. In the latter approach, pupils individually at random will be asked to answer. This does lack the at random procedure, but will give the teacher some idea of how well pupils are achieving. In general discussions, each day, the teacher also may notice who responds and who does not. All need to be brought into the discussion, if at all possible. Each item stressed in teaching and learning situations, may be recorded by the teacher and then a random sampling of what has been taught may be selected for writing the test items.

Periodically the teacher might wish to give the same test over again in a few days to notice reliability, or consistency of measurement for each pupil. From standardized tests, validity and reliability data are provided in the Manual of the company publishing the test (Ediger, 2012).

REFERENCES

Ediger, Marlow, and D. Bhaskara Rao (2012), *Curriculum and School Teacher*. New Delhi, India: Discovery Publishing House.

Ediger, Marlow (2009), "Issues in the Social Studies" *Experiments in Education*, 37 (4), 75-78.

Ediger, Marlow (2012), "The Psychology of Teaching Mathematics," *Delta K*, 50 (1), 20-21.

2

Relevant Issues in Curriculum

There are salient issues in the curriculum which need resolving. These issues involve key concepts in curriculum development which affect learner achievement. Teachers, curriculum directors, and school administrators must study the pros and cons of each indepth Time will need to be given to this important endeavor in shaping objectives, learning opportunities, and appraisal techniques (Ediger, 2009).

Issues in Curriculum Development

First, to be sure, effort is salient in pupil achievement. Too frequently, Learner A attempts to get by with as little effort as possible. Others, including Pupil B put forth much effort and does not succeed with the task at hand. There is wasted time in either of these two situations. Learner A needs motivational strategies with different materials of instruction plus encouragement/assistance. Pupil B may need to use a different approach in mastering an algorithm, for example, in mathematics. Effort, no doubt, has an end which then requires reevaluation and change of course. Consider, too, whereby an individual selected a job/vocation which was over his/her head. Otherwise, effort is indeed a valuable attitude in goal attainment.

Second, interest, also, is a valuable trait in that it increases opportunities to do well in different subject matter areas. Teachers need to secure interests of pupils in order to achieve objectives of instruction. It is marvelous if the interests are there, already, or can be developed in any lesson/unit of study. There are times when an interest is too narrow as in dinosaurs solely/largely, and then interests need to be broadened in scope. Pupils must explore different facets of knowledge and skills to do well in diverse curriculum areas, or for purposes of choosing a future vocation or job.

Third, sequence in learning is poignant in that pupils build upon previously acquired facts, concepts, and generalizations in order to tackle the ensuing objectives of instruction. Who should ascertain proper order or sequence in learning, the teacher or the learner? The teacher might utilize measurably stated objectives, developed on the state or federal level. These objectives are developed by specialists in their academic fields of endeavor and also correspondingly with aligned mandated tests. With the objectives, if behaviorally stated, the pupil is either right or wrong in his her responses. The aligned tests, too, are multiple choice test items as a whole, in which responses are objectively scored. With machine scoring, a plethora of tests are scored in a very short period of time. Thus, the teacher as well as the writers of state/ federal objectives and test writers determine, in large part, sequence/scope in pupil learning.

Toward the other end of the continuum, constructionism as a psychology of learning which stresses the saliency of pupils largely determining the order of learnings to be pursued. The teacher becomes a guide and facilitator. The Hutchinson, Kansas News (April 12, 2013 issue) contained an article of a Sterling, Kansas High School senior who developed a cookbook of recipes used by a local custom wheat cutting crew of her parents. The crew each summer followed the wheat harvest as it ripened in the area to be cut. This high school senior, as a baby, cared for by her parents would travel with the crew. The recipes were compiled in book form, along with information on travels made during the wheat harvesting season. It took time and effort to complete the project. Once the project had been decided upon, the high school senior, supervised by the instructor, was involved in sequencing her own activities toward project completion. This project did not involve the use of measurably stated objectives to achieve, nor testing to ascertain progress. The project stressed personal progress made in achievement. The completed project incorporated the work of the student which might well have included the following facets in its total appraisal:

- neatness in its undertaking
- thoroughness in the project
- clarity in writing and grammatical usage
- appropriate sequence of content.

Fourth, high expectations of pupil work in different academic areas is elaborated upon rather frequently in educational thinking, it is good to assist pupils to achieve optimally. Hastily done, careless work, and a lack of effort is to be frowned upon. Pupils do need encouragement and help to do well in school. The problem arises as to how high the expectations should be. The following exaggerate the concept of high expectations:

- going beyond what is truly reasonable for learner achievement
- omitting pupil decision making as to what is reasonable
- complete teacher determination of the curriculum

It certainly is good pedagogy if teachers work with pupils to secure quality work in all of learner endeavors. Reasonable high expectations make for sound pedagogy.

Fifth, equity versus excellence has received much attention in the educational literature. The goal in equity is to minimize/eliminate achievement gaps between and among the races. Black students, in particular, should be assisted to eliminate this gap. There is talent within all racial groups and this must be cultivated. It is a waste of human ability not to achieve well. This is a noble idea to put forth with teacher effort to attempt to eliminate gaps in achievement between and among the racial groups. However, I feel that in trying to do away with the gap, gifted and talented pupils might all be held to a similar level of achievement. My beliefs are whatever the contributions to be made should be optimal from each and all groups. By doing this, each person has chances to achieve optimally and contribute as much as possible in any academic discipline. Teachers and school administrators need to be aware of and be held accountable for the welfare and optimal progress of each and every student.

Sixth, getting along well with others in collaborative situations is highly poignant. Thus, small group endeavors must be emphasized in teaching and learning situations. Committee formation must make pupils feel they belong and are successful. Being on a committee with one who harasses is not enjoyable to say the least. Thus, guidelines must be followed whereby each participant is respected and contributes fully, but does not dominate the small group. Valid and reliable consensus or conclusions must be realized. Knowledge and skills are necessary in collaborative endeavors and need thorough assessment. Knowledge may be evaluated in terms of accuracy, completeness, and being sequential. Skills of learners might well be appraised as to :

- stressing clarity of expression
- staying on the topic
- appropriate order of content being stressed
- helping others in developing a sense of belonging
- thinking critically and creatively to solve problems (Ediger, 2013).

Evaluation of Achievement

There is a plethora of issues involved in the evaluation process. A major issue pertains to the amount of credit to be given to pupils based on daily school work as compared to standardized test results. In the past few school years, passing a standardized test has almost been the gospel in promoting pupils from one grade to the next as well as ratings given to schools. What about everyday work of pupils in the different academic disciplines? There are pupils who do well in testing situations while others feel more motivated to reveal progress in ongoing lessons and units, There needs to be rational balance between the two.

There is also an issue pertaining to how teachers should be evaluated. There are educators who believe that pupil test results should be a salient part of the assessment. Others believe that there are too many variables, other than teaching, which enter in to the equation, pertaining to pupil test results.

Recently, there have been advocates of school principals being evaluated, in part, based on learner test results. Here, there are indeed many factors, other than principal leadership, which enter into test results of pupils.

Concluding Statements

There are numerous issues in the school curriculum which need resolving. Teachers, school administrators, and parents, as well as other interested persons in education, need to communicate effectively with a planned, series of meetings to seriously identify key issues in curriculum development with major attempts made at achieving resolutions.

REFERENCES

Ediger, Marlow (2009), "Issues in the Social Studies," *Experiments in Education*, 37(4), 75-78.

Ediger, Marlow (2013), "Teacher Observation to Evaluate Mathematics Achievement," Is, 12(10), 3-5.

3

Changing Role of School Principal in School Curriculum Implementation

The role of the school principal has changed much in the recent intervening years. Thus, he/she was formerly thought of as a manager and management of the local school. Management is poignant, but being a leader in improving teaching and learning situations is more salient. Leadership is needed to provide the best experiences for pupils in the school setting. The instructional objectives need to be relevant and possess clarity. Vague statements, ambiguous in nature, have little value in teaching and learning situations. Then too, varied learning opportunities for pupils to attain objectives should be motivating and challenging; appraisal procedures need to be valid and reliable. Standardized test results are limited in what they measure. A variety of approaches must be utilized including everyday teacher observation of learner obtained knowledge and skills.

The Principal as Leader of Curriculum Improvement

School principals must believe in pupils being able to achieve optimally in school and in life. Thus, reasonably high expectations need to be in the offing.

Pupils are human beings who have definite needs in life which must be met. They need to have adequate nutrition such as school breakfasts, lunch, and dinner. The latter has not been met by most schools unless they have an after school program of quality learnings. Weekend food packs to take home provide learners with some nutrition needs over the weekend.

There should be a clothes closet in the school setting to provide suitable clothing for those in need. Cooperation with agencies in society should be stressed to secure necessities for all, including school supplies.

The principal must advocate collaborate endeavors in different curriculum areas to promote pupils having belonging needs met. These endeavors must truly emphasize pupils accepting each other with positive feelings involved. No one likes to be an isolate and be shunned by others.

Pupils need to feel they possess worth, and principals need to assist teachers to recognize accomplishments of learners. In everyday lessons, the teacher may notice improvement of a learner over previous performances in mathematics, science, social studies, reading and the language arts, as well as citizenship behaviors. These need to be recognized and thus, each pupil might receive recognition. A brief statement of honest praise such as "that's fine" may suffice. Different words and phrases might well be judicially utilized in the recognition process for pupils to have esteem needs met.

Communication between communicator and communicated need to be clear, concise, and accurate. Poor communication hinders with pupils failing to secure directions, explanations, and conveyed information (Ediger and Rao, 2013).

Principals must become self-efficacious in knowledge and skills in curriculum development. There are selected areas in which principals may play leadership roles in assisting teachers in teaching and learning situations; among others, the following are examples:

In reading, teachers need to assist pupil :

- use of context clues, as well as selected learnings in phonics as the need arises.
- utilization of phonics in initial consonant recognition in word identification. Additional phonic elements may be added as necessary.
- application of *close* reading skills so that learners truly understand ideas in reading comprehension.

- ability to read critically and problem solve.
- use background information to attach meaning to the ensuing reading lesson.

In mathematics, teachers need to guide pupils to :

- acquire and attach meaning to structural ideas.
- utilize reasoning and inductive methods of achievement.
- think analytically and engage in problem-solving.
- being creative in the use of algorithms.
- use in different levels of complexity as to the commutative, associative, and distributive properties in mathematics.
- diagnose and remediate in daily lessons and units of study.
- sequence learnings to accommodate algebra, and geometry in a K-12 order.
- preparation of students for college/the work place.

In science, pupils need to experience :

- high quality experiments and demonstrations, directly related to ongoing lessons and units of study.
- higher levels of cognition whereby analytic, synthesis of ideas, objectivity, and creative thinking are emphasized.
- close reading of science content is in evidence. Rereading and verification of content are salient goals.
- writing experiences in science need to reflect accuracy, meaning, and completeness.
- oral communication must be thorough and convey meaningful subject matter with clarity, as well as respect and acceptance of others.
- resilient behavior, efficacy, responsibility, and effort must be stressed (Ediger, 2010).

In Social Studies, pupils need to experience :

- primary and secondary sources of information.
- class as a whole, committee, and individual endeavors with collaboration and positive interaction with other learners.
- project methods in planning, sequencing, and assuming responsibilities for completion and evaluation.
- written work involving doing quality summaries, outlines, narrative accounts, essays, persuasive products, and descriptive writings.
- contributing optimally in discussions when engaged in committee endeavors.
- giving of oral reports involving good sequence, clarity of expression, appropriate voice modulation, and gaining attention of listeners.

The school principal is the leader in the school involving improvement of the curriculum, and he/she must accept that responsibility in a diligent manner. The following are inservice education opportunities for all teachers, as well as the principal self-involvement in acquiring self-efficacy:

- workshops and faculty meetings.
- attendance at state and national educational conventions including the National Association of Elementary School Principals.
- doing a research project pertaining to a facet of improving the curriculum.
- working toward an advanced university degree in school administration.
- reading and discussing recent journal articles, published by the National Council Teachers of English, International Reading Association, the National Council Teachers of Mathematics, The National Science Teachers Association, the National Council for the Social Studies, the Association for Supervision and Curriculum Development, the National Association of Secondary

School Principals, and the National Association of Elementary School Principals. These publications should be housed in the professional library in the school setting for easy access.

REFERENCES

Ediger, Marlow (2010), "The Pupil, Writing, on the Science Curriculum", *Experiments in Education*, 38 (4), 19-22.

Ediger, Marlow. and D. Bhaskara Rao (2013), *Curriculum and School Teacher*, New Delhi, India: Discovery Publishing House Pvt. Ltd..

4

Role of Supervisor in Curriculum and Instruction

The duties and responsibilities of the curriculum supervisor have changed much over the years. Seemingly, rapid changes are occurring at the present time. The curriculum does not remain static, but is subject to change due to a plethora of changes in society. Technology, for instance, is indeed making for changes with innovations being brought into the classroom making for workshops and faculty meetings, among others, in updating the curriculum. Making changes, hastily, must be avoided; they need to be implemented with much thought and deliberation. Technology and its use must be brought into teaching and learning situations, if other approaches are less satisfactory.

There are numerous approaches and methodologies, based on sound educational research, theory, and practice, which must be tried out in providing for more optimal pupil achievement. Feedback, based on these practices, provide information for teacher use in ensuing pupils activities and experiences (Ediger and Rao, 2013).

The Innovative Curriculum

With continual study, analyzation, and inservice education, the classroom teacher may assist in providing for individual optimal pupil growth and achievement. The supervisor of the curriculum must stay abreast and be updated on the latest trends in teaching and learning.

There are selected principles of learning which encompass all curriculum areas in the school setting. These include the following:

- ample opportunities need to be given to learning by discovery procedures. Here, the teacher guides learners to find information on their own with minimal assistance. The learning by discovery approach may be utilized in problem-solving and project methods, in particular.
- accurate, clear communication of ideas be it in giving directions, conveying needed information, or in different facets of lesson/unit teaching. The spoken voice must be well modulated with proper stress and pitch as well as enunciation.
- proper sequence needs to be in evidence with within each learning activity. With problem-solving and project methods of instruction, the pupil, largely, sequences his/her own learnings with teacher guidance. With deductive methods of teaching, the teacher must notice that ideas and explanations provided are orderly, so that pupil knowledge acquired might be based on previously achieved ideas.
- pupil purpose needs emphasizing. Thus, the learner perceives reasons for achieving. This is different than memorization for test taking whereby the pupil regurgitates subject matter. Purpose for learning goes more in the direction of the learner sensing that content/skills are relevant in school and in society. It is the pupil who needs to achieve objectives of instruction with the intent of using what is being acquired in ensuing situations. Relevancy is then being stressed in the curriculum.
- the interests of learners must be gained in order for more optimal attainment to occur. These must not be disconnected from ongoing activities, but rather active involvement needs to be in evidence. Interest provides for effort in developing, growing, and achievement. Effort makes for increased energy levels for learning.

- meaning in learning is salient. With meaningful content/abilities, pupils understand that which is being focused upon. Meaningful subject matter/skills has transfer values to new learning experiences. Proper attitudes might well result in that positive feelings toward learning accrue.

Thus, the supervisor of instruction must be well versed in the psychology of learning and be able to assist teachers in utilization of these inherent principles. When engaging teachers to offer help, the supervisor emphasizes quality human relations and realizes the saliency of transactions may be hindered due to rudeness, being aloof, abrupt, and unkind. Assisting teachers in realizing and accepting innovative ideas involves an inward desire in making changes. These cannot be forced nor accepted through authoritarian methods. Good communication involves stressing accuracy and rational thought on the supervisor's role in guiding teachers to move from traditional procedures to what is new and inviting. This is a complex task when teachers are holding on to a strong traditionalist point of view, but supervisor persistence and perseverance might well make for change in a desirable way. When modifications do occur, it becomes rewarding to both teachers an the supervisor of the curriculum. The consequences of changes made should increase pupil achievement and satisfaction in the classroom.

Supervisors need to know teachers as individuals and not as impersonal beings. Thus, the supervisor shares, not only the best ideas in teaching and learning but also his/her interests, hobbies, and goals in life. Personal relations must be improved upon to make for a school culture of learning. This might well open the doors for classroom teachers to share what is salient in their personal lives. Communication needs to be open for ideas to flow in curriculum improvement. This is also important when thinking of school/pupil, and parent relationships. It is poignant for teachers to visit homes of pupils and notice the home setting environment. Good human relations are of utmost importance in these situations. Thus, teachers need to learn more about the pupils they teach and involve parents in the education process of their offspring. How parents can help children to love school and learning is of utmost importance. For example, there is much parents can do to assist pupils in different curriculum areas such as:

- reading aloud to young children and discussing illustrations in these books with children. Pointing to words as they are being read aids the child to identify abstract words in reading. the read alouds also help pupils acquire general and specific knowledge and skills.
- taking pupils on excursions to nearby places and discuss what transpired.
- assisting pupils in naming objects when going to a place of interest, such as a supermarket. Vocabulary growth is of utmost importance.
- doing simple science experiments with children. Let the child identify the problem, develop an hypothesis, and draw a conclusion.
- listening to and discussing news items on the child's level of understanding.
- writing a friendly letter, cooperatively, with the child. Discuss briefly each necessary part of the letter.
- play listening games in the home setting (Ediger, 2007).

Parent/teacher conferences might well be an excellent method of communicating with the parent. These must emphasize good will. Work products of the pupil should be available to evaluate the present status of the child's achievement as well as discussion of future goals to attain. There is a plethora of things to elaborate upon in parent/teacher conferences which include specifics such as problems a pupil faces in reducing fractions and, in general, including citizenship behaviours, working collectively with others, decision-making, anger management, among others. Notes may be jotted down and utilized for the next conference in noticing changes in the child's behaviour. Communicating regularly with parents is salient and may also be done through the following approaches:

- e-mail messages in reporting continual progress
- letters mailed through snail mail
- brief conferences by means of mobile or landline phones
- parent/teacher organization meetings
- school night where teachers are introduced by the principal to parents in a large group session with ample opportunities later to meet the child's teacher.

Collaborative endeavors are salient for pupils to assist in meeting the goal of getting along well with others. This is salient now as well as in the future workplace. Teachers need to place learners in a committee setting which fosters good human relations. Where antagonism is in evidence, changes in committee membership must be made so that cultivation of quality attitudes might persist and grow. As pupils grow in improved human relations, a more heterogeneous group may be formed to achieve goals in the curriculum. Four to five members in a small group makes it possible for all to contribute frequently. The teacher must model for pupil observation what good human relations would look like and mean. Thus, learners need to respect the thinking of others, have ideas circulate within the small group so that each might contribute, be polite and eliminate rudeness, as well as work toward objectives attainment.

Teachers, also, will need to work in collaborative endeavors in developing new curricula or modify that which exists. The supervisor, too, must be involved in inservice education. Thus, the following criteria should be followed:

- staying on the topic
- clarifying ideas presented, as necessary
- avoiding interrupting others during discussions
- emphasizing quality sequence and coherence
- presenting cogent ideas
- developing and using relevant criteria to assess achievement.

A variety of procedures need to be used to evaluate pupil achievement. Mandated valid and reliable standardized tests are one approach. However, teachers should not drill learners for the purpose of ranking high on these tests. Rather, quality principles of teaching must also be emphasized in the instructional arena. Drill and rote learning make for memorization which is not conducive to developing good attitudes toward each academic discipline, nor does it help in retention of subject matter.

Standardized test results must be utilized with other methods of assessment such as teacher evaluation of everyday achievement of pupils. What pupils do every day in each lesson needs to be appraised. Thus, attitudes, work and study habits, citizenship behaviors, and pupil empathy must also be assessed. Anecdotal records must be kept by the teacher for each pupil in the ongoing curriculum.

In Conclusion

The role of the curriculum supervisor is changing rapidly and modifications in teaching and learning situations need to be made. However, changes should not be made for the sake of doing so, but to emphasize improved objectives, learning activities and evaluation procedures. Each child deserves the best in education to be ready for career and college. At the same time, learners need to enjoy learning as well as have basic needs met of nutrition, sleep and rest, proper clothing, and safe shelter. Belonging needs and recognition for being valued for its own sake must be stressed.

REFERENCES

Ediger, Marlow (2007), "Meaning in Reading Instruction," *Reading Improvement*, 44(4), 217-220.

Ediger, Marlow, and D. Bhaskara Rao (2013), *Curriculum and School Teacher*. New Delhi, India: Discovery Publishing House Pvt. Ltd.

5

Philosophies of Reading Instruction

There are selected philosophies of reading instruction which are relevant in providing for individual differences among learners. These need to be studied indepth by reading teachers in order to best provide for each pupil in the classroom. Pupils differ from each other in reading achievement, interests, and purposes, and it is a challenge to assist each child to become the best reader possible in achieving objectives of instruction.

Approaches in Teaching Reading

State mandated objectives and tests have become salient. These are developed by those at the state/federal level who are removed from the local school district. They attempt to ascertain what pupils should know and be able to do at certain levels in the child's public school experience. These specialists are not familiar with and do not know pupils who actually will be tested. The test results are strictly preserved and used in high stakes testing to determine who will be passed on to the next grade level. A single test given to all in a selected grade level determines who will be passed and who will fail. The advocates of mandated testing basically utilize:

- multiple choice test items with a stem and four possible responses
- the test writers are assumed to be correct in judgements made in writing each to measure learner proficiency
- pilot studies need to be made to develop validity and reliability standards
- many test items can be written with machine scoring

- printouts provide feedback from each pupil's results to provide information to the teacher on what needs further emphasis in teaching, based on test results
- answers given by pupils, generally, are either right or wrong.

There are reading specialists who believe that setting standards for pupils to attain is the way to go in teaching and learning situations. Some feel that teacher salaries need to be construed, in part or whole, based on pupil test results. Tests then should determine a pupil's future at a university or work place. What is generally omitted in the equation is that motivated learners, as well as the late maturers, can overcome obstacles, and make up lost learnings, and do well in university occurs work. Individuals, of course, have been successful in the world of work, without doing well in school. There are weaknesses in testing advocates' thinking:

- measurement is a philosophy education and is predicated on the corporate model, such as ascertaining the growth or lack thereof of sales to the lay public.
- human minds are different in that flexible principles of learning are involved in teaching and learning situations.
- there is much that tests fail to measure well or minimize in evaluation such as interest in subject matter, human relationships, and resilience.
- it fails to take into account pupil's relevant questions and identified problems, unrelated to what is on a test.
- teachers teach toward what is on a test which has then omitted important curriculum areas such as social studies, art, music, and physical education (Edigerand Rao, 2012).

Mandated testing is quite important in the nation in that governmental officials and leaders in academic fields can hardly think of education without testing and measuring pupil progress.

Somewhat toward the other end of the continuum is the philosophy of personalism which greatly minimizes the saliency of measurement and testing. Here, the teacher has a wide variety of library books, attractively arranged, from which a learner may choose sequential books to read. If a pupil is not able to make a selection, the teacher is there to advise on a choice based on that person's interest level. The teacher becomes a supervisor, aid, and assists pupils when needed in word recognition. After the learner is through reading a library book, he/she may have a short conference with the teacher to appraise word identification techniques when reading a passage orally. Comprehension is also emphasized in that the teacher and pupil might discuss characterization, setting, and plot, or general interest in the book. The conference is dated and a short list jotted down on accomplishments and remediation needed to be referred to in future.

The reading teacher then observes pupil attention to the task at hand and records observations made for the class as a whole as each learner pursues personalized reading. The teacher is a guide in that

- assistance is provided in library book selections as the need arises
- help is given pupils in developing reading and comprehension skills
- he/she develops an environment of making reading an enjoyable experience with attractive bulletin board displays indicating fascinating library books to read
- introductions to selected newly arrived books is made to whet appetites for personalized reading
- learner attitudes toward books is commonly assessed (Ediger, 2012).

The reading teacher needs to work closely with parents in securing the letter's cooperation in developing pupil interest in reading. Thus, parents need to have an ample supply of library books in the home setting. These may be purchased or checked out from the school or public library. They need to read aloud, informally, to young children as soon as attention is given to the oral activity. The young child, however, should not be forced to pay attention and must be respected. Presenting and discussing ideas with children is always a good idea if done enthusiastically and with respect. When children are in the public school years, it is still good to read aloud to them in the home setting. However, selected youngsters become good readers at an early age and may wish to read silently to themselves. There are high school students who do not do well in reading and are hindered in academic achievement due to a lack of salient skills in word recognition, which then leads to comprehension difficulties. For these students, it is good if in the home setting, a parent reads aloud a required school selection while the student follows along in the textbook. Discussing what has been read aloud assists the learner to attach meaning to printed content. Reading should be as enjoyable as possible to encourage the student to do more reading in different academic areas of course content as well as reading for relaxation and pleasure.

Attending parent/teacher conferences is highly significant. Here, the parent and the teacher may evaluate the offspring's progress in reading as well as make plans for future reading activities and achievement. Criteria to follow include the following:

- accepting the thinking of others
- discussing ways of helping the learner overcome identified difficulties
- ascertaining which books are of interest to the child
- suggesting appropriate library books for the child to read
- making a plan, cooperatively, to assist pupil progress in reading achievement
- securing pupil input into likes and dislikes in reading library books.

Conclusion

There are either sides of the continuum in the debate of predetermined objectives/tests mandated by the state or nation versus more of pupil self-selection of reading materials in the local public schools. There is also a plethora of in-between points of view. Perhaps, this might best be mediated by looking at as wells appraising the following factors:

- which procedure best meets the needs of individual pupils?
- might the two be harmonized in providing for the "best of all possible world?"
- how can pupils motivation in desiring to read be increased?
- do reading teachers have a preference in which plan they, individually, would like to implement due to personal teaching strengths?
- which plan has the better chance of securing pupil interest in reading?
- is pupil purpose a viable choice in ascertain the selection of a reading programme?
- how might pupil vocabulary development best be strengthened?
- which approach best measures/evaluates learner achievement and progress in reading instruction?

REFERENCES

Ediger, Marlow (2012), "The Great Debate in Reading Instruction," *Reading Improvement*, 40(2), 19-22.

Ediger, Marlow and D. Bhaskara Rao (2012) *Essays on Teaching Reading*. New Delhi, India: Discovery Publishing House Pvt. Ltd.

6
Wither Reading Instruction?

In time, the teaching of reading changes in its objectives, learning opportunities, and methodology. Teachers of reading need to stay abreast in occurring trends and issues. It behooves the teacher to attend workshops, professional meetings, and discuss with other teachers what should be emphasized in teaching and learning situations, among other approaches in curriculum improvement.

Innovation in Reading Instruction

Close reading is salient for optimal pupil achievement. Thus, learners need to reread subject matter, when needed to realize objectives of instruction. It might be that the individual fails to understand content at a given point in reading a selection and needs to go back to extract meaningful content in a paragraph. Understanding what has been read is poignant! Survey approaches are not sufficient in selected situations to achieve meaning. Thus, indepth procedures must be emphasized when different purposes are stressed in reading. In part, this can be attained with rereading what was not understood from the printed materials. This is generally done to locate answers and solutions to problem solve. It also might be stressed to verify information. Comprehension of subject matter is vital and indepth learning is energizing in this manner. Effort on the part of the pupil is just as salient as abilities in ongoing learning opportunities. The reading teacher then must motivate pupils to achieve in ongoing activities and experiences. Energy levels for learning are increased through motivation.

The reading teacher needs to be able to teach, effectively, the different levels of pupil achievement such as the gifted, talented, average achievers, slow learners, minority children, and the mentally deficient. Thus, feelings of self-efficacy can come about with opportunities for growth in teaching reading by doing the following:

- taking reputable courses online
- attending classes and working toward an advanced degree from an accredited university, in the teaching of reading
- doing an independent study on a facet of reading instruction such as critical and creative thinking
- participating in a specific grade level inservice education programme in the local school district
- discussing problem areas in reading instruction with colleagues and the school supervisor
- engaging in a study to determine the kinds of errors pupils make in reading
- attending state and national conventions pertaining to the teaching of reading
- speaking at the local parent/teacher organization meeting on involving parents/guardians in improving reading instruction.

Teachers need to assist pupils in word recognition when necessary. When a pupil is stuck in recognizing a word, context clues must be emphasized. Thus, a pupil needs guidance at that point to fill in a word which makes sense in relationship to the rest of the words in the sentence or paragraph. In some cases, this is adequate in coming up with the correct word in context. If this is not adequate, then the involved pupil needs to sound out the initial consonant of the unknown word which then should correctly identify what was an an unrecognized word. Subject matter read is salient when emphasizing comprehension of content, and identification of unknown words must not take the joy out of reading. As an alternative, a word which is not known to the reader may be quickly identified/pronounced by the teacher or a good reader in the classroom. Additional procedures in word recognition techniques might be the following:

- use of picture clues, especially for young readers whereby illustrations are more abundant in their reading materials
- phonics, as needed in achieving independence in reading.

Social and emotional learning needs to be interwoven within teaching and learning situations. Rudeness, bullying, and put downs hinder learner progress. A classroom environment must be in the offing which facilitates learning to read. Thus, classroom rules need to be developed and maintained. Infracture of these rules requires effort of the involved pupil to correct the deficiency. Harmonious relationships need to exist between and among pupils and the teacher. Pupils need to be respected as well as the classroom teacher needs to receive respect. This makes it so that the teacher can teach and pupils can learn. Causes for misbehavior need to be sought, if possible, and these may include :

- pupil hunger and/or fatigue
- problems in the home setting such as quarreling and dissension
- pupils striving to receive attention through negative approaches
- negative teasing, rudeness, and inappropriate treating of others
- inadequate feeling of belonging to the group and classmates.

For the first asterisked item above, hunger needs are met, in part, by school lunches and breakfasts, but dinner needs may be unmet unless the school has a quality after school programme with food needs met at that time. Asterisked item #3 indicates that esteem needs should be met and thus encourage positive behaviour. Praise for improved performance in the classroom and school surroundings need adequate attention and provided for each pupil. Asteristed Item #4 should emphasize a war against bullying with careful monitoring of behaviour. Item #5 stresses the importance of learners having pleasant experiences in committee and collaborative school experiences. This does not eliminate or minimize pupils putting forth much effort in achieving.

There are a plethora of additional traits which pupils need to develop to accomplish or reach toward proficiency in reading. In supervising university student teachers in the public schools, the writers noticed that perseverance does help to make for success in reading. Too many pupils in the classroom fail to concentrate on word recognition and want immediate assistance in identifying the unknown. The unwillingness to take time to "figure out" these unknown words makes learners more dependent upon others. Pupils need to be taught to be as independent as possible when reading subject matter or narrative accounts. To persevere means to continue on a task until completion. This might well be accomplished with teacher assistance as well as encouragement. As much as possible, hindrances in comprehension of content read should be eliminated. Perseverance is a remarkable trait in school and in society (Ediger, 2012).

Self-discipline is another trait which needs encouragement. Reading teachers must supervise pupils to the point whereby they discipline the self to accomplish objectives of instruction. Approximately, thirty per cent of the classroom time is wasted and should rather be spent on reading accomplishment. This can be done with teacher modeling and consistently drawing the pupil's attention to pay attention to the task at hand. Reading achievement is systematic and sequential with more optimal effort put forth!

Success in reading is also based on resilience factors of the involved pupil. Being able to "bounce back" from failures is important. Much of life involves "recouping" from mistakes and errors. It is only human not not be prefect, even though efforts are there to achieve well. Reading teachers need to discuss what resilience means and how it affects human progress. Individuals tend to worry too much when traditional mistakes are made, and instead need to move forward in achievement of life's goals.

Perhaps as salient as any objective for pupil acquisition is self-regulation. A lack of this is observed in many situations such as in anger exhibited. If unregulated, people say things that are ordinarily rejected and cause embarrassment. This causes difficulties in thinking in a forward manner in making progress in the task at hand. Self-regulation is highly important in reading instruction in the following ways:

- pupils avoiding distractions in the classroom and pay attention to ensuing lessons
- concentration on reading subject matter and narrative accounts, presently being emphasized, and not thinking of other things such as what to do on weekends
- staying with doing a reading project until completion. Opposite is giving up readily or doing inferior work
- making definite efforts to stay alert during time devoted to large and small group reading instruction as well as in individual endeavors
- assisting collaborative reading endeavors to be successful and not disrupt this salient learning opportunity
- asking for teacher assistance when necessary in independent and other activities involving reading
- doing meticulous written work in the reading/writing connection (Ediger and Rao, 2013).

Teacher Leadership in Improving the Reading Curriculum

In addition to the school principal providing leadership, classroom teachers, also, need to lead in this direction of improving instruction. Thus, a primary grade teacher took an approved leadership role in leading her teachers to examine standardized test results to notice what needs to be taught and retaught in first grade critical thinking. They researched educational journals, teacher education university level textbooks, as well as other relevant print materials. Agreed upon ideas were tried out in the respective teacher's classrooms and the results reported to the group for comments. Evaluation of progress thereof is salient to notice, as well as modifications which need to be made. If headways are made and the involved teachers have feelings of satisfaction, the group will, no doubt, continue to meet to look at other problem areas. Members need to develop

- a passion for problem-solving
- support each other in pursuing problems to solve
- respect each other's thinking in an atmosphere of respect
- achieve feelings of belonging to a relevant group of professionals
- a desire to share with peers vital information relating to improving the reading curriculum
- develop feelings of wanting to promote good reading practices in the community.

REFERENCES

Ediger, Marlow, and D. Bhaskara Rao (2013), *Curriculum and School Teacher*. New Delhi, India: Discovery Publishing House.

Ediger, Marlow (2012), "Literature in Social Studies, the Pupil, and the Teacher," *Journal of Instructional Psychology*, 39(2), 80-82.

7

Reading in an Integrated Curriculum

Reading instruction needs to be useful across the different curriculum areas. It should not benefit only one academic discipline, but have relevancy in all materials read in school and in society. Reading is a highly valuable skill in school work, at the work place, as well as for recreational purposes. A wide variety of genres should be available for pupil reading to capture interests of learners. In this way, pupils, too, may latch on to what is important in decision-making within life's endeavors. Then too, the total development of the learner is involved when supplying books dealing with cognition, and the attitudinal dimension. Thus, it is more than content acquisition, but also encompasses social and emotional learning.

Reading Across the Curriculum

Word recognition techniques are useful in reading from different academic areas. There are several approaches which might be utilized in solving problems in word recognition when engaged in the act of reading. One procedure is for the class or small group to read together from an enlarged projection in which all can see the contents clearly. With a brief introduction providing readiness for reading, the teacher may read aloud together with pupils as he/she points to each word being read. This may be repeated as needed so that pupils identify words correctly in sequence. This might be time consuming if utilized repeatedly with beginners, struggling readers, and those who are having difficulties in remembering ensuing words. Thus, using context clues in words which present problems in recognition provide a plan for identification. If a pupil is "stuck" on a word, he/she may provide a word which makes sense and is meaningful in relationship to other words in the sentence or paragraph. Sometimes, a learner provides a word which is outlandish and does not make sense and this can be pointed out to the pupil. Narrowing it down to a meaningful word eliminates/minimizes what is not appropriate. It might then be necessary to bring in phonics with looking at the initial consonant in pronouncing the ensuing word. This procedure usually is adequate. If more aid is necessary, additional letter sounds may be brought to bear upon the unknown word. Additional procedures to use include the following:

- using picture clues, especially for younger children in which numerous illustrations appear per page. If a pupil does not identify a word, the illustration might assist in or identify the unknown.
- using phonetic analysis in associating sounds with symbols or letters.
- using a glossary or grade level appropriate dictionary, although this might slow down sequential comprehension.
- using peer assistance in recognizing unknown words.
- the teacher writing the new words on the chalkboard for all to see clearly and going over these words, until mastery, with pupils in developing a sight vocabulary.

Indepth comprehension is very salient in reading subject matter. This is opposite of survey procedures. Thus, rereading might be needed when seeking answers or solve problems form reading text materials. Problem-solving requires an hypothesis related to an identified problem. The hypothesis needs testing and rereading may assist in accepting, modifying, or rejecting the stated hypothesis. Verification of plausible solutions needs indepth comprehension of reading subject matter. In problem solving across the curriculum, reading of content is one approach in reaching a tentative solution. Technology utilization is also important when reading subject matter from internet sources! In writing up summaries, the word processor might well present content clearly and neatly. Pupils need to have an adequate spelling vocabulary in order to use spell check. If words are spelled too outlandish, spell check may be of little value (Ediger, 2010, pp. 46-52).

Skills and abilities in reading comprehension are stressed in critically analyzing ensuing subject matter. Thus, content must be separated in terms of accurate from inaccurate information. Too frequently, pupils determine answers to questions from personal opinions possessed rather than conscientiously seeking out what is more accurate. Too let go of erroneous opinions and reach out toward the more accurate requires flexibility. Flexible thinking, too, is needed to sort out what is biased from that which is more accurate. Reading teachers need to demonstrate flexibility of thought and emphasize this in teaching and learning situations. Again, the verification principle is in operation here with the use of reputable printed materials. With a plethora of television programmes and narrative accounts stressing imaginative accounts in their programmes, it behooves the teacher to help learners focus upon factual accounts when seeking accurate subject matter. What has then been read needs to be summarized into a relevant conclusion. The conclusion must hold "water" and not be leaky as a sieve. This was strongly stressed to me in an undergraduate English class whereby Essays from a basal text were read by students enrolled the course whereby in class the main idea or ideas were considered as presented by college students. It involved critical thinking to ascertain if a conclusion/main idea stood the test of encompassing, broadly, an entire essay. There was considerable discussion in coming up with a '"water tight" generalization. The same approach might well be used in age appropriate materials read by public school pupils. Flexibility is needed in making the adaptation. Badders, National Science Teachers Association President (NSTA, 2013) wrote the following pertaining to reading across the curriculum:

"Since many goals are the same, where are the opportunities for a teacher of science to incorporate reading and writing into inquiry based science instruction? Some possibilities include, but are not limited to, searching and gathering information, in nonfiction texts, making sense of scientific data, taking notes, teaching concept mapping and working with vocabulary.

Using nonfiction and informational text can also be the vehicle for teachers to address the teaching of text features that are needed not only in science, but also across the disciplines. Understanding how one uses a table of contents, an index, a glossary, diagrams, illustrations, captions, bulleted lists, headings/subheadings and special type characteristics such as bold, are critical strategies for improving reading instruction."

Plans of Reading Instruction

There are diverse plans of providing reading instruction across the curriculum. Individualized reading emphasizes an array of library books on different reading levels being available for pupil choice. The teacher assists in the choosing if a learner cannot select a book to read. Time during the day needs to be set aside for individualized reading. The books deal with diverse genera pertaining to history and the social studies, science, and mathematics, among other bodies of knowledge. Thus, a pupil may choose to read a library book on Plants and Animals since this unit title is being emphasized in class. Or, the learners might select a book on Living in Japan, since this is of great interest to the child. In my experiences as university supervisor of student teachers in the public schools, pupils may read about the Changing Surface of the Earth from different reference sources including the internet and present subject matter during regular class time for discussion on that topic. Pupils show much interest in this procedure. Each pupil presents information as the need arises during discussion time. Rules are elaborated upon and heeded to when evaluating processes involved in having a good discussion.

Content in the basal textbook might also be used in securing major generalizations and main ideas. Background information leading to content in the text needs to be obtained, prior to its reading. The following procedure is recommended here:

- find out through questioning what pupils already know on the topic
- write questions down for all to see what learners desire to find out when discussing the related illustrations in the textbook
- while this is being done, list the new words in the ensuing reading on the chalk board or utilize the white board for this purpose. Give learners practice on these words until mastery occurs.
- have pupils read to locate answers to asterisked items three and four
- reread for accuracy and verification of information found
- emphasize quality criteria for discussions
- help pupils to reflect upon in information found with stress placed upon critical and creative thinking as well as problem-solving
- implement the project method in order to assist learners in using what was learned, as well as encouraging indepth learning (Ediger, 2010, pp. 117-119).

In between procedures (individualized reading versus basal textbooks) might also be used. Both then become salient if :

- balance is developed and maintained between the two approaches
- pupils indicate success in reading achievement
- basals are used in more formal approaches in instruction such as in teaching word recognition techniques, whereas individualized reading stresses increasing enjoyment in reading endeavors.

Appraisal of Progress

There are several approaches which might well be used in the evaluation process and include :

- reputable standardized tests
- quality teacher written tests and teacher observation
- checklists and rating scales
- pupil self-evaluation in terms of standards
- project evaluation as related to subject matter read.

REFERENCES

Badders, Bill (20113), "Linking Science and Literacy," *NSTA Reports*, November, 13.

Ediger, Marlow (2010), "Children's Literature in the Science Curriculum," *Journal of Instructional Psychology*, 37(2), 117-119.

Ediger, Marlow (2010), "Psychology of Parental Involvement in Reading," *Reading Improvement*, 45(1), 46-52.

8

The Changing Reading Curriculum

With the oncoming Common Core State Standards (CCSS), reading instruction will change in time. New objectives and measurements of achievement are to be in evidence. Much greater emphasis on critical and creative thinking is to be stressed, along with other modifications. Inservice education for teachers, based on CCSS guidelines professionalizes teaching. Pupils feel more challenge as they progress through the public school years. The overall goal is to secure readiness for careers and college, upon graduation from the public schools.

The New Reading Programme

CCSS emphasizes higher levels of cognition in teaching reading. Increased emphasis is to be placed on information books and less on narrative accounts. Proper balance between the two are then needed. Thus, critical reading stresses pupils analyzing content read. Information type textbooks stresses pupils reading for main ideas in separation from subordinate content in order to obtain a structure of information. Subordinate subject matter is related to and support the main idea. Rote learning and memorization are lower levels of thinking and need to be exchanged for higher orders of thought. Thus for example, pupils may compare and contrast two different sources of information on the same topic to notice likenesses and differences. Or in narrative writings, pupils may be asked to notice and elaborate on character or setting differences between two accounts.

Rereading might be necessary numerous situations to verify arguments and debates among learners. Close reading is then stressed and may be contrasted with survey procedures in reading. Too often, subject matter is read hastily without obtaining the gist of what a writer is expressing. By reading content carefully and going back to what was not understood, the pupil attaches meaning to the ongoing experience.

Failure to identify selected words when reading makes for a lack of close reading as well as a lack of comprehension. Comprehension in its diverse manifestations is the reason for reading. Teachers in subject matter disciplines need to be teachers of reading. If a pupil is "stuck" on reading a given word, he/she must possess a methodology of word recognition. The following may be stressed in teaching pupils:

- **use of context clues.** If a pupil cannot identify a word, he/she needs to fill in with a word which makes sense in relationship to other words in the sentence or even paragraph.
- **use of phonics.** Sounding out selected letters, in addition to the use of context clues, especially beginning consonant letters in an unknown word.
- **use of picture clues.** Books for young children, in particular, may have numerous photos and the unknown word problem might be solved with the viewing of the illustration.
- **use of teacher assistance in rather immediate word recognition.** Thus, the teacher pronounces the unknown (Ediger and Rao, 2012).

Word recognition problems should be solved as soon as possible so that the learner does not lose sequence of subject matter read. Reading skills achieved need to cut across all academic areas. To reiterate, comprehension of subject matter is the goal of reading diverse kinds of literature. The following are given as examples, beyond that of critical and creative reading covered previously:

- Quoting accurately from the materials read when responding to a question. Inferential thinking is poignant here in that between the lines reading is salient. Careful reading and developing accurate generalizations is important.
- Analytical reading is necessary when the learner separates major ideas from supporting content. This aids pupils in focusing upon what is vital as compared to that of lesser value.
- Comparing the meanings of words from one type of subject matter to another. These meanings may be recorded in the pupil's notebook as well as be placed on a word wall in the classroom. Pupils tend to look at the word wall during leisure time. Metamorphic as well as literal interpretation may be emphasized.
- Contrasting content from the same/similar genre read to notice style, theme, and point of view. Read literature from different genre to broaden interests and purposes in reading.
- Perceiving how a narrator's point of view has influence over the total subject matter contents. It is poignant for pupils to identify how the point of view might slant contents in the written work being studied.
- Noticing beauty of language and interpretation of different kinds of poetry read. Rhyme and syllabication need to be stressed as well as meter and rhythm.
- Understanding, in depth, of subject matter read. This might be noticed in small and large group discussions, valid and reliable essay tests, and in personal written work.

Inservice Education of Teachers

A carefully planned programme of inservlce education needs to be in the offing so that teachers become thoroughly knowledgeable of Common Core State Standards (CCSS). They must understand the objectives emphasized and the "whys" of CCSS. Possible learning experiences also need an in-depth study. These should reflect the thinking of the psychology of learning. Discussions must also cover diverse evaluation techniques to ascertain what pupils have learned (Ediger, 2007).

REFERENCES

Ediger, Marlow, and D. Bhaskara Rao (2012), *Essays on Teaching Reading*. New Delhi, India: Discovery Publishing House Pvt. Ltd.

Ediger, Marlow (2007), "Meaning in the Reading Curriculum," *Reading Improvement*, 44(4), 217-220.

9

Rereading Information Sources:

The Textbook

Reading textbook information has been done too superficially in the past. More time needs to be given to its indepth comprehension. Thus, a new emphasis in reading has come about. What was stressed previously has been modified to incorporate pupils thoroughly comprehending the subject matter presented in an ongoing reading activity. Learners will then be accountable for understanding subject matter read intensively. Survey reading will then be replaced, unless there is a specific need such as skimming in an index or table of contents or for a specific purpose.

Reading in the Curriculum

In reading information sources, replacing some of the over emphasis in narrative content, the teacher needs to be certain that pupils are reading for meaning. Formerly, pupils experienced much background information, known as readiness for reading, but the feeling was this was overdone. Readiness experiences, of course, are still salient when relating the old with the new subject matter to be read. However, this must be delimited to what is needed. Too frequently, the readiness activity has been extended excessively. The same is true of word recognition skills whereby these should be taught as necessary but not dominate the reading curriculum. The focal point for the learner is to read to obtain cognitive knowledge. Understandings obtained here will transfer to many topics in reading across the curriculum (Ediger and Rao, 2012).

Questions raised in reading information sources generally require more careful reading of the selection in finding answers. Evidence must be cited to substantiate answers. This involves meticulous reading of subject matter. Thus, many answers may be derived from the text selection being read. The answers to questions might also come from other reference sources, but the initial textbook content needs a pupil focus which requires reading to develop main ideas, supporting ideas, as well as facts. Comprehension of subject matter then receives a different approach which stresses rereading and verifying content read.

Utilization of subject matter, in addition to discussing and elaborating on its contents, may be emphasized in diverse learning activities such as :

- doing a reader's theater involving learner planning and implementation
- summarizing main ideas and supporting subject matter
- writing and performing a play with committee input
- reading related subject matter and developing conclusions therefrom
- giving an oral report on a chosen topic
- doing a creative dramatics presentation without play parts.

Indepth learning then becomes paramount. Critical reading is a salient factor in rereading. Thus, learners need to be guided in thinking critically to separate facts from opinions, accurate from inaccurate content, as well as separating major from minor ideas. Reading to secure answers to questions as well as to solve problems, also, requires adequate time spent on conscientiously ascertaining which are poignant as well as the unimportant subject matter read to secure needed answers and solutions. Careful thinking is vital in these situations.

Creative thinking also needs attention in that the pupil should come up with novel, unique ideas related to the ongoing reading activity. These library books encourage reading and the motivation to read what is vital in obtaining subject matter from information texts. The following, among others, might assist in motivating creative thinking skills:

- careful reading of Dr. Suess′ books such as Green Eggs and Ham
- reading poetry which includes free verse, limericks, quatrains, haiku, and triplets
- the classroom teacher reading his/her written poems to pupils
- using metaphors and similes for pupils to emulate in creative writing.

Pupils must read and reread subject matter in order to secure objective content from the writer of a selection. Along the way, learners need to develop skill in word recognition. Automaticity is then involved when recognizing sequential words in a reading selection. Automaticity occurs when pupils have experienced adequate skills in reading fluently which involves :

- use of phonics, picture clues, and context clues in identifying unknown words
- possessing a rich reading and speaking vocabulary
- paying attention to punctuation marks e.g. periods, question marks, exclamation points, commas, capital letters, among others
- relating reading to writing
- reading orally with expression and with the author's intent
- reading for a variety of purposes (Ediger and Rao, 2005).

Fluency in reading is an ultimate goal. If pupils read information sources fluently, improved opportunities for quality comprehension might well occur. With fluency, pupils are not hindered in word recognition problems. Reading too becomes :

- more enjoyable in the school setting which precludes leisure time reading
- a highly skilled endeavor, with more reading emphasized in school and in society, further refinement of skills tend to occur
- a definite part of attitudinal development. Positive feelings tend to increase toward reading across the curriculum
- a highly prized activity whereby time is made available for personal experiences in reading.

Reading Across the Curriculum

When reading a larger number of information sources well, the learner will become more conscious of a need to increase vocabulary since each academic discipline may have its own unique terms. These must be meaningful and make sense in context. Thus, pupils need to increase vocabulary strengths. A major reason learners do not attach meaning to academic subject matter is that they have minimal understanding of inherent vocabulary. Word walls in the classroom is one approach in assisting pupils to understand vocabulary terms. Thus, new words are seen and reviewed on the word wall. The writer when supervising university student teachers in the public schools noticed many times how pupils in leisure time would go to the word wall and concentrate thereon. It appears that pupils try to learn and retain learnings longer in vocabulary with the word wall. They tend to utilize new words in discussions on subject matter read. Dictionary and glossaries are also excellent to use in vocabulary development, but it does take up time to look up each vocabulary term as contrasted with word wall use, However, learners also need to develop skill in using these, among other tools or resources in learning.

In closing

Pupils do need to attain objectives which emphasize achievement in order to be ready for higher education or work place endeavors. The time to start a quality reading curriculum is in nursery school with its readiness experiences and going up to college/university or be ready to function well at the work place. This means that the classroom teacher needs to be cognizant of how to group learners for instruction in reading as well as:

- provide sequential activities
- provide a variety of interesting experiences to capture learner attention
- provide evaluation results (formative and summative) to guide instruction
- provide diagnosis and remediation as needed
- provide for psychological needs of learners such as belonging and esteem. Thus, the feeling dimension of learners is important to emphasize

REFERENCES

Ediger, Marlow, and D. Bhaskara Rao (2005), *Teaching Reading Successfully*. New Delhi, India: Discovery Publishing House.

Ediger, Marlow, and D. Bhaskara Rao (2012), *Essays on Teaching Reading*. New Delhi, India: Discovery Publishing House.

10

Teaching Reading and the Common Core Standards

The common core standards emphasize a kindergarten through secondary school progression and will apply to all students in the nation. National tests then measure pupil progress. They are different from the No Child Left Behind (NCLB) law in that the latter stressed that each state develop their own tests to measure pupil achievement, making it impossible to notice how well pupils did nationally. NCLB then emphasized ascertaining pupil progress based on separate tests for states individually. Thus, one state may have easier or more complex tests than did the other(s).

The question arises, "How might learner attainment be optimized in reading in order to attain higher test scores ?"

Motivating Common Core Learning

Pupils need to be motivated to achieve needed knowledge and skills in reading. For young children, the following word attack skills need mastering:

- using picture clues, as well as selected learnings in phonics as in initial consonants to recognize words
- using context clues, patterns in words, and syllabication analysis as needed in word identification.

Comprehension of subject matter should include obtaining main ideas and subordinating content, cause and effect thinking, and problem solving procedures.

The above word recognition skills as well as comprehension strategies serve as a basis for future success in reading and in attaining common core objectives. Each ensuing objective builds upon previous learnings. Background information is needed in subject matter as well as in skills to achieve as optimally as possible in acquiring progression in reading. The new objective must be attained as seamlessly as possible when relating the new with previously achieved objectives. Additional objectives which need attention include the following as learners achieve progress throughout the school year:

- critical reading in separating facts from opinions, accurate content from the inaccurate, and fantasy from reality
- creative reading in coming up with novel ideas, uniqueness of thought, and originality
- problem solving strategies whereby the reader generalizes from data given in answer to a dilemma situation
- reading/rereading to attain vital concepts
- reading between the lines and verifying content from within the selection being read
- reading directions to develop a project in an ongoing unit of study (Ediger and Rao, 2012).

Reading should be a useful and a practical curriculum area in school and in society, and in attaining common core objectives. Classroom teachers must provide ample time for silent as well as oral reading. In oral reading, teachers may discern the kinds of errors made by individual pupils. These might well become a basis for instruction in small and large groups if errors are somewhat persistent to most learners. Otherwise individual assistance might well be given as the oral reading progresses. Errors (miscues) may consist of not being able to identify a word, giving an incorrect substitution, hesitating in word recognition, lacking fluency in reading, omitting words, among others. Each miscue needs identification and remedied with patience as well as quality instruction.

Silent reading should be stressed during reading instruction as well as in sustained silent reading. The latter emphasizes each pupil choosing a library book to read toward completion. If a pupil is not able to settle down with reading a library book, the teacher may suggest one which harmonizes with that pupil's interests, and achievement level. Periodically, a conference may be held with the reader to appraise skills in word recognition and in comprehension. The point being that children need to read library books at home and in school. They become good readers through reading which helps in word identification as well as in comprehension. The home setting can do much to aid in the goal of reading progress by reading aloud with enthusiasm to offspring and providing honest praise for effort put forth by children. A variety of library books should be available to children in the home setting. These may be purchased and/or secured from the public library.

Being a good reader is necessary in school and in society at the work place. Well paying and responsible jobs/ professions require high quality abilities in reading. Throughout the secondary school years, more reading of abstract materials is emphasized; thus reading readiness needs to be sequential from the elementary school years and upward. Thus, students need to hone skills in critical and creative reading, reflective thought, problem-solving, as well as reading analytically. Self-efficacy is highly significant in that the student feels confident to face tasks of the future. Leaning upon the self and engaging in quality decisions making abilities is salient (Ediger and Rao, 2013).

To engage in more complex skills in reading, high school students need to have ample opportunities to engage in the following, among others:

- reading for a variety of purposes in classes taking in different curriculum/academic disciplines
- taking part in and writing school plays and reader's theater

- doing much writing, directly related to course work, and proofing of written work
- writing poems for publication with assistance provided by consultant teachers
- being a member of the school newspaper writing team
- increased reading for leisure and enjoyment
- rereading a selection to increase accuracy in comprehension.

Common Core State Objectives can be achieved with a high quality schedule in reading.

The amount of reading done on the higher education level is indeed great. It is amazing in selected college/university courses that a student is able to complete all the complex reading required in a semester! It must be a major objective of all teachers/instructors to stress the saliency of reading. All teachers need to be teachers of reading regardless of the title of the course taught. For those attending technical school, reading skills are vital in all endeavors of work. The writer, for example, when attending a rural high school, 1942-1946, engaged in much reading when taking three years of vocational agriculture. These were good experiences for one who is highly academic, being vice president and president of the local FFA Chapter, being third high in the state FFA livestock judging contest, as well as being awarded the State Farmer degree open to two per cent of the members within the state. Perceiving the saliency of reading in all of life's endeavors assists in attaining common core objectives.

Narrative reading will not be omitted, but stressed on the primary grade levels. Sequentially and on through the secondary years of schooling, identification of characters and the setting of the narrative, the sequence of the action, the plot, and theme will be emphasized in literature classes. By doing much reading and using the inherent tools necessary for word recognition and comprehension of content, the pupil will improve fluency and interest. Information kinds of reading together with narrative content assists the learner in becoming a good reader. Exciting discussions (See Vygotsky, 1978) which motivate and inspire pupils assist in doing more reading for diverse purposes. Vocabulary growth and development must be ongoing and continuous, not only in literary works but also in science, social studies, and mathematics, among other curriculum areas.

In Conclusion

The common core state standards should enhance pupil achievement and development in order to be ready to succeed in college/university courses as well as at the work place after high school graduation. Readiness for these goals may well be enhanced through the CCSS.

REFERENCES

Ediger, Marlow, and D. Bhaskara Rao (2012), *Essays on Teaching Reading*. New Delhi, India: Discovery Publishing House Pvt. Ltd.

Ediger, Marlow, and D. Bhaskara Rao (2013), *Curriculum and School Teacher*, New Delhi, India: Discovery Publishing House Pvt. Ltd.

Vygotsky, Lev (1978), *Mind and Society*. Cambridge, Massachusetts: Harvard University Press.

11

Reading Achievement and Pupil Progress

There are many recent high goals that have been set for pupils to attain in reading. For example, when being a student in the public schools, 1934-1942, an illiterate person was one who could not read, period. Now, the expectations are much higher in that many politicians and educators have set as a goal that all third graders read on the third grade level, or higher, when completing the third grade. Is that possible? Probably not. There are too many factors which enter in for all to attain the third grade baseline, such as pupil abilities, home environment, encouragement from parents, among others. What might a modern reading curriculum look like in assisting learners to achieve well in reading?

Reading, the Pupil, and the Teacher

First of all, each pupil must have basic needs met in nutritional foods, suitable clothing, safe and clean homes, friendly neighbourhoods which are accepting of children, suitable clothing, medical and dental help, and a school setting whereby learners feel they belong and are valued for their own sake. Seemingly, each person also desires to have esteem needs met for qualities and behaviours possessed.

Schools have done much to meet these needs including the serving of breakfasts, lunch, and a packet of food to take home for the weekend. However, this stills leaves dinner needs unfulfilled unless an after school program is in evidence which includes the evening meal. Meals served during the summer vacation is a necessity. Summer school, also, with high quality teaching can do much to assist learning in being sequential. During the summer months, much forgetting might occur and learning experiences may well remedy this situation. Needed is public school pre-kindergarten for three and four your olds taught by well qualified teachers possessing a degree in early childhood education (ECE) from an accredited university (Ediger and Rao, 2012).

The above are definite to fulfil if learners are to become good readers. Certainly, children will attain more optimally in reading if the above named needs are met. An ensuing programme of high quality experiences with a recommended innovative reading curriculum should aid in upping progress. Pupils need to experience high, but reasonable expectations. Success in a challenging reading programme is of utmost importance. Scaffolding must be utilized by the teacher to assist learners to move from where they are presently in progressing to a more ideal level. The scaffold is achievable and definitely not making for failure. Failure leads to a lower self concept and this is opposite of being successful in reading instruction. Building improved self concepts is salient to be successful presently as well as at the future workplace.

Learning opportunities to achieve objectives need to create interest in reading. Wholehearted involvement in the diverse activities should provide for individual differences so that each pupil might attain more optimally. Questions raised and problems identified during ongoing lessons require dose reading. Thus, a learner may need to reread the selection to secure valid answers to questions or to check hypotheses. Verification is poignant and, in many cases, comes from the text. Argumentation for an answer/solution might also come from another reliable source. Too frequently, hazy and vague discussions have occurred from reading subject matter; clarity must be stressed. Additional information sources may be utilized, as necessary, to check answers and hypotheses from the ongoing discussion. An increased emphasis needs to be placed on reading information texts, rather than narrative accounts, due to academic subject matter being emphasized, more heavily, as pupils move progressively through the different grade levels.

In beginning reading instruction, as well as in in higher grade levels as is necessary to aid pupils in becoming better readers, phonemes and phonics should be taught in context to help pupils associate symbol and sound. In diagnostic teaching, it may be revealed by learners that they have not mastered the different sounds making for phonemes or there is a lack of making the connections between letters and individual sounds when identifying unknown words. Comprehension of subject matter is the ultimate objective of instruction in reading. This involves knowledge/skills in phoneme identification as well as utilization of phonics to aid in recognizing unknown words. The use of context clues provide an additional approach in word identification. The following might also be used in identification of unknown words:

- use of picture clues, especially for young readers when the pictorial is utilized rather heavily in reading materials.
- utilization of words in bold print or italics which pinpoint salient vocabulary terms to master. Sometimes these words are defined in context and provide a phonetic spelling.

Comprehension of content needs to stress indepth teaching; survey approaches are not recommended since shallow subject matter may soon be forgotten. Thus, the reading teacher needs to use a variety of learning experiences whereby reinforcement of learning is in evidence. Critical thinking is important whereby the pupil analyzes fact from fiction, the relevant from the irrelevant, as well as the accurate from the inaccurate. Pupils need ample time to reflect upon subject matter read, and in doing this, use is made of subject matter. Further uses are made in doing a project or in problem solving.

Upon reflection, learners, too, might well come up with novel responses for creative endeavors such as doing a mural or writing a poem pertaining to that which was read. After analyzing subject matter, the pupil is then lead to synthesizing content whereby a conclusion, summary, or product is developed.

Collaborative endeavors might well be used when comprehension of subject matter is being emphasized. Small group discussions, carefully arranged in terms of membership, may then choose a literary problem to be solved. The problem needs clarification, be relevant, and incorporate learner interest. Leadership might emerge during the discussion, instead of appointing a leader. An appointed leader might also be chosen if this works more effectively. Members need to stay on the chosen topic and not digress. Each member must be encouraged to participate in the discussion, and no one should dominate. A free flow of ideas in the collaborative setting is desired. Too frequently, ideas move from one member to the chairperson, back to a member, and then back to the chairperson/leader, and then to a different member of the discussion group. Rather, content should move freely within the committee membership. With adequate background information, pupils should be able to move ahead on their own during the discussion; the teacher always needs to be available for encouragement and providing ideas as needed. The teacher is a guide, supervisor, and helper, but not a lecturer nor continuous dispenser of information. Committee members during the discussion may :

- evaluate ideas presented in terms of standards
- assist each other to move forward during the committee endeavor
- help in making vocabulary terms, concepts, and ideas meaningful (Ediger 2007).

Quality oral communication is valuable within discussion groups. To be effective members, pupils need to develop self-confidence in language use. Proper stress, pitch, and enunciation should be practised to notice its affects on listeners. A monotone voice has a tendency to turn off listeners. A well modulated voice, speaking at an appropriate rate of speed, can do much to enhance good listening. Pupils need practice in giving different kinds of speeches including to inform (like presenting book reports), to describe how something was done such as developing a model, and/or tell of reasons for doing a project such as collectively making a mural. Quality oral communication is a valuable asset in school and in society. It transcends/involves all curriculum areas.

Good written work is also valuable as it integrates a curriculum, being very valuable in each academic area. Pupil purpose for writing is salient in that perceived reasons should be in evidence for participation. The question needs answering pertaining to the following: What use can be made of the written communication? Thus, if a learner cannot see any reason for writing, little effort will be put forth. Motivation tends to be lacking in these situations. The teacher must think of activities which will motivate pupils in the writing experience. Writing of ideas needs to be sequential and related in each paragraph. Generally, they will refer to and present content on the topic sentence. Sentences within a paragraph usually possess a subject and predicate. Pronouns are words used in place of a noun. Modifiers (adjectives and adverbs) should be taught in expanding each sentence to make for clarification, as well as interest. Prepositions are few in number and introduce an adjective or adverb clause. Conjunctions may be taught as connecting words, phrases, or clauses of equivalent value. Interjections may be recognized with an exclamation mark which reveals strong feeling. The study of grammar is sequential and needs to be taught as it relates directly to the writing activity. Memorization is not recommended, but each part of speech may be taught meaningfully as the need arises. Grammar/writing can be an interesting topic. Too frequently, it lacks interest and fails to motivate learners. Grammar is abstract, but can be made concrete with purposeful writing experiences. The following are guidelines to use in grammar instruction:

- make connections with writing across the curriculum
- use lifelike experiences for written work, such as writing a letter to parents/guardians telling about a personal learning experience in school

- emphasize the part/parts of speech as the need arises to clarify ideas presented
- stress the utilization of grammar as being real and reality based
- implement the concept of pupil comprehension of grammar being taught
- sequence learnings in teaching grammar in context, showing its worth.

Conclusion

Objectives must be carefully selected for pupil attainment. They need to be challenging and achievable. Learning experiences need to be varied to meet objectives achievement. Interest needs to be inherent in learning. Valid and reliable evaluation procedures provide feedback from the learner to the teacher, for ensuing learning activities.

REFERENCES

Ediger, Marlow (2007), "Meaning in Reading Instruction," *Reading Improvement*, 44(4), 221-223.

Ediger, Marlow, and D. Bhaskara Rao (2012), *Essays on Teaching Reading*. New Delhi, India: Discovery Publishing House Pvt. Ltd.

12
Meeting Pupil Needs in Reading Instruction

In selected situations, funding for public schools has declined draconically. In a few states, for example, income taxes will become a thing of the past. Only state sales tax and property taxes are then available to support public schools. No attempt is being made to find a substitute for state income tax as a revenue source. Something will have to give. Reading instruction will suffer in these situations as a part of the cutback. This would be most unfortunate since a high quality public school education is needed for everyone. Positions, jobs, and professions require higher levels of education and training for entry level work.

Instead the public school educational ladder must be extended downward to include pre-kindergarten experiences for all. Well qualified teachers are needed for all pupils. This would aid those who are in the disadvantaged category to receive background experiences that children have in a rich home environment.

High Quality Reading Instruction for All

Pupils need to experience word recognition skills which assist in identification of the unknown. If learners do not receive assistance in identifying the unknown words, they tend to gloss over what does not make sense. In the meantime, comprehension suffers. It is, of course, much better to help pupils become independent readers. Thus, the reading teacher must guide pupils to use context clues in that the supplied word makes sense in relationship to other words in the sentence or paragraph. It is easy to evaluate if a pupil supplies a word in place of the unknown which does make sense. If this is not adequate, the pupil must view the first letter, or letters if it is a digraph, in attempting to use phonics in word recognition. Practice should be given to retain the correct recognition of the previously unknown word. Additional phonic leanings might well be emphasized as needed. These need to be selected carefully so that word recognition skills increase sequentially. The ultimate goals in phonic instruction and word recognition skills is to improve comprehension in securing relevant subject matter content. The following might also be utilized to aid in word recognition:

- *use of picture clues*. The child, then, might not be able to identify an unknown word, but the related picture on the page being read provides the necessary clue.
- *use of configuration clues*, in that the shape and form of the word provides some indication of its correct identification.
- *use of phonic spelling, in parentheses*, given by the text writer, may provide needed hints.
- *use of direct definition of a word provided*, by the content writer, to increase comprehension.

Reading comprehension may be analyzed into component parts and each needs to receive its proper emphasis. Critical reading is very valuable in school and in society. Here, the individual, for example, separates facts from opinions in problem-solving situations. Facts are necessary as solutions to problem solve. Then too, creative thinking is needed in order to come up with unique, novel ideas. Creativity provides for originality of ideas which are needed to move forward in the societal arena. Innovations and inventions have brought on changes in how work is done involving less manual labour. To reiterate, other purposes include the following:

- reading for a sequence of ideas as in time frames involving history
- reading to secure a summary or conclusion

- reading to obtain a main idea
- reading between the lines for needed information
- reading to locate specific facts and information
- reading for purposes of synthesizing information
- reading pictures to secure vital subject matter.

Reading and writing are definitely related; the connections between the two must be strengthened in the curriculum. A purpose may be to take salient notes on acquired subject matter. Use is then made of what has been written. Further purposes in the reading/writing connection are the following:

- writing a book report
- writing an outline on a chosen topic for use in reporting to the class
- writing diary entries summarizing what was learned in ongoing lessons
- writing a log pertaining to a summarization of diary entries
- writing a self-evaluation in terms of criteria on unit work
- writing sequential steps to follow in doing a project (Ediger and Rao, 2012).

There are selected standards to follow in written work and these need to be achieved developmentally. Thus, proper grammar and punctuation need to be in evidence. Correct spelling of words if spell check or long hand is involved in the written work. Order of subject matter must be sequential. In most cases, a sentence needs to contain a subject and predicate. It is salient to avoid misplaced modifiers such as adjective and adverb clauses. Punctuation marks including periods for declarative and imperative sentences, question marks for interrogative sentences, and exclamation marks for exclamatory types of sentences. Achievement and progress must be appraised in terms of where the pupil is presently with reasonable progress to be expected. Rubrics may be developed and utilized to evaluate written products.

The skill of listening is poignant in all curriculum areas. Pupils need to show continuous improvement in being good listeners. Standardized tests to measure listening achievement are available; however, the teacher might keep dated anecdotal statements pertaining to the quality of listening for each pupil in the diverse academic disciplines. Subject matter and skills must be presented clearly, using proper voice inflection. The teacher, too, needs to notice if pupils in the classroom setting are ready to listen with adequate background information, and are not distracted with objects on or in the desk. Pupils who distract or enjoy entertaining others need to be brought back into the fold, ready to listen to ongoing activities. Periodically, the teacher needs to have pupils sequentially restate the directions which were given for a specific lesson. This is to check listening quality. Everyone loses out in learning when being distracted. The following are listed that need to be evaluated which hinder good listening habits:

- pupils who turn off and are bored with the present activity.
- improper seating arrangements. Thus for example, two disrupters should not be seated next to each other.
- preventable and unnecessary noise.
- not meeting the learning styles of individual pupils.
- not using the psychology of learning in teaching pupils.
- lack of teaching materials which fail to meet personal needs of learners.
- objectives that are too difficult to achieve (Ediger, 2007).

REFERENCES

Ediger, Marlow (2007), "Learning Activities in the Curriculum," *College Student Journal*, 41(4), 967-969.

Ediger, Marlow, and D. Bhaskara Rao (2012), *Essays on Teaching Reading*. New Delhi, India: Discovery Publishing House Pvt. Ltd.

13

The Teacher of Reading and the Child

Reading instruction is in a state of change with emphasis being placed upon Common Core State Standards (CCSS). Inservice education is necessary with teachers moving toward implementation of these standards. CCSS stresses pupils in Kindergarten through grade twelve, upon completion, being ready for college or careers. This is truly a salient undertaking and will take a high quality scope and sequence programme of instruction to do so, particularly, in reading and the language arts. The contents of this manuscript will deal with the reading facet of CCSS. How will the teaching of reading differ?

Specific Emphasis of Reading Under the Common Core

More emphasis is to be placed information content with a somewhat lesser stress upon narratives. Close reading is a very relevant concept for teachers in that very careful attention is to be paid by children on vital subject matter on sequential pages. Questions raised might well be answered and verified by content read. The answers might well be found on a page which may require rereading. Indepth study is necessary here. Survey procedures are not recommended nor is skimming at this point. Achieving a central idea or ideas is salient for pupils when reading and rereading subject matter indepth. These main ideas assist pupils to develop structural content. The structure of subject matter provides a framework for ensuing experiences in reading. New ideas might then be related to the structure and provide a broader scope in the main idea.

Vocabulary can cause pupils to misunderstand what is read unless clarification occurs. Attempts to clarify may come from teacher guidance in helping pupils reason what the contextual meaning is. It becomes a reasoning process in coming up with meaning being attached to the vocabulary term. Pupils need aid to becoming independent in word recognition in order for fluency to come about. This, too, involves using context clues to determine the unknown word. Here, the pupil with teacher assistance reasons what a correct word would be that fits in with the other words and the paragraph in the sentence. Phonics, also, needs adequate attention. Meaning is inherent here in that sense must be made of what has been read. Rereading of text materials utilized assist in developing clarity of meanings within the framework of teaching and learning situations (Mueller, 2005).

Reading emphasizes questioning by pupils and the teacher for accuracy of understandings. To receive answers to questions might well require probing, covering textual materials. Higher levels of cognition are needed to stress the thought processes in questioning. Probing requires indepth thinking, not hasty unknown products. Then too, critical thinking is in the category of indepth thinking, might be more time consuming in that facts need to be separated from opinions, fantasy from reality, as well as accurate from inaccurate ideas.

Reflective thinking stresses the saliency of rehearsing/ reviewing indepth to obtain deeper meanings from a text being read. This is done to identify different questions as well as to secure increased information. Less forgetting occurs if ideas are brought to the attention of the involved learner; the result should be to integrate knowledge with fewer ends. This might well relate directly to the structure of knowledge of an academic discipline.

Diverse kinds and types of literature to be in the offing such as poetry, drama, short stories, diverse genre, and novels as the developmental level of the learner progresses. Poetry, for example, should be enjoyed in its reading with reflection upon the beauty of language Thus, words expressing onomatopoeia or echoic sounds provide a basis for using creative terms which mimic sounds such as in a rainfall Metaphors and similes make creative comparisons in poetry such as "The clouds in the sky appear as sheep roaming around" compares the "sky" with "sheep roaming around." Alliteration, another poetic element, stresses two or more sequential words beginning with the same sound, such as "round robin" or "Suzie sings." Identification of poetry with both ending words rhyming is a couplet; three lines with ending words rhyming is a triplet; whereas four lines of rhymed verse is a quatrain.

Non-rhyming poetry include free verse. Those with a certain number of syllables per line include haiku with three lines respectively having five, seven, five syllabi words per line; tankas have a five, seven, five, seven, seven syllables each per line for the five lines. Poetry needs to be comprehended in meaning along with its rich extended vocabulary. Close reading of poetry, too, is needed to include depth teaming (Ediger and Rao 2012).

REFERENCES

Ediger, Marlow, and D. Bhaskara Rao (2012), *Essays on Teaching Language Arts*. New Delhi, India: Discovery Publishing House.

Mueller, K. (2005), "Creating Zones of Possibility for Struggling Readers," *Journal of Literacy Research*, 36(4), 419-450.

14

Change and the Mathematics Curriculum

As society changes, the school curriculum also needs innovations, and modifications, mathematics included. Numerous study groups have been involved in making needed changes including the National Council Teachers of Mathematics. The content and methods of teaching loom large in teaching and learning situations. Which are needed modifications in this endeavor?

Key Mathematical Concepts in Teaching

Structural concepts and generalizations are of major importance. These provide the framework for pupil's understanding of fundamentals in mathematics. Pupils may reveal meanings of structure when acquiring selected properties of number such as the commutative and associative properties of addition and multiplication. These properties of number are attained meaningfully within ongoing lessons and units of study, and are used at increasingly levels of complexity.

Mathematics teachers need to stay abreast of major facts, concepts, and generalizations in their areas of academic specialty. Subject matter knowledge comes in handily when teaching pupils developmentally as well as remedially. Pupils need to be taught by competent teachers who possess feelings of self-sufficiency whereby they feel comfortable in teaching pupils of diverse ability levels, socio-economic levels, and interest differences. With knowledgeable mathematics teachers, pupils are encouraged to study, explore, and achieve, regardless of individual differences. Each child is motivated to learn due to high quality instruction.

Models must be utilized to assist in understanding key concepts. Computerized as well as actual physical models may be used in the instructional arena. In context and sequentially, pupils, for example, may observe cylinders, cones, pyramids, triangular solids, cubes in three dimensions, as well as plane figures including squares, rectangles, rhombuses, circles, among others. These need to be observed carefully and discussed, using the senses of sight and touch. Indepth teaching is necessary to notice likenesses and differences. Generalizations from each concept must be acquired through reasoning and discussions. Accuracy is a poignant criterion to use in mathematics instruction. Vagueness, as well as expressions of haziness, must be changed or modified. Mathematics represents an academic discipline which possesses objectivity, patterns, and rules which are a significant facet of teaching and learning (Ediger and Rao, 2011).

Problem-solving as learning opportunities are salient to emphasize in ongoing mathematics lessons and units of study. These problems are relevant in that they are poignant and useful in school and in society. If these are word problems, for example, in a basal textbook, the teacher needs to be certain that pupils recognize the abstract words, making for meaning and fluent reading. When supervising university student teachers, I noticed that pupils may work word problems incorrectly due to a lack of required skills in reading. There are several approaches which might well remedy these situations:

- read aloud word problems together with the pupil, pointing to each word orally being pronounced
- the teacher explaining, briefly, the salient contents to those who have reading problems
- the teacher or a good reader assisting with word identification by using context clues and necessary phonic learnings to identify the unknown

- use a committee setting whereby members assist each other, if help is needed, in word recognition inherent in problem-solving
- make certain that pupils attach meaning to new words encountered. These words in mathematics may be placed on a word wall for pupils to see and discuss
- make a booklet of mathematical terms.

Reasoning from evidence must be stressed in teaching and learning situations. Reasoning needs to be critiqued and arguments must be viable. This involves abstract and quantitative reasoning. Pupils need to study and analyze the critiques and thus attain reasonable conclusions. Critical thinking is involved in separated the rational from the irrational, the accurate from the inaccurate, as well as major from minor ideas. Thus, diverse kinds of thinking are important in ongoing units of study. Learners need to look for regularity in reasoning with repeated consistency. Patterns need to be expressed in diverse lessons which provide background information to pupils for ensuing units of study. Mathematics has structure, consistency, patterns, and repeated reasoning.

Much is being developed in technology for mathematics teaching. Technological means of instruction are costly to purchase and to service. Updating technology is a constant problem. However, wisdom in decision making pertaining to needs involved require thought, knowledge, and reflection. The goal is to assist pupils to achieve more optimally in the mathematics curriculum, and not purchase equipment for the sake of doing so. Thus, for example, computers and software programmes must stress the following:

- high quality objectives to be stressed
- saliency of sequence advocated
- motivational factors to stimulate learning
- clarity of mathematical subject matter and ideas
- readiness for learning factors

- achieving pupil interest in the curriculum
- structural ideas emphasized (Ediger and Rao, 2009).

Committees of competent teachers need to be involved in choosing necessary technology. The investment is made to aid to attain overall goals of pupil numeracy.

There are several groups on the state/federal levels who authored/edited mandate objectives for learner attainment. Related tests, too, have been in the offing from these groups. The last group of which 46 states have signed onto their programmes is the Common Core State Standards (CCSS). They have as goals/objectives to prepare students from Kindergarten through grade twelve and be ready for college/work place upon high school graduation. This is quite an undertaking! Whether or not this truly provides what pupils need for success remains to be seen. CCSS will be implemented during the 2014-2015 school year.

No Child Left Behind (NCLB) federal law, passed in 2002, is still being implemented with its requirements of students being promoted to the next grade level upon passing a one shoot mandated test. Thus, in grades three through eight, pupils are promoted if test results are satisfactory. One part of NCLB has been eliminated/minimized is the Adequate Yearly Progress (AYP) section which caused difficulties in many school districts due to students testing "proficient" by the 2014 school your.

Mandates come and go with each attempting to be better than what was experienced previously. The writer benefited much from the National Defense Education Act of 1958 (NDEA), passed one year after the then Soviet Union, now Russia, sent up the first space ship to orbit the planet earth. The Federal government then paid for one-half the cost of teaching materials in mathematics, science, and foreign language instruction, which had to be approved by the State Department of Education. As a school administrator, the writer's school district developed a good science laboratory. Through NDEA funds science, mathematics, and foreign language instructors completed advanced degrees in these academic disciplines. The NDEA focused upon improving instruction through the increase of approved teaching materials as well as in inservice duration. Many teachers received NDEA moneys in order to complete advanced university degrees.

NCLB has not been renewed by Congress, but is still a part of federal law. CCSS is coming into being during the 2014-2015 school year. The latter emphasizes the same standards for all pupils in the United States while NCLB has different standards in state to state comparison.

An important item pertaining to mandated testing is that they be :

- valid in that what is measured pertains to what has been taught
- reliable in that the tests are consistent in indicating what each pupil has learned.

REFERENCES

Ediger, Marlow, and D. Bhaskara Rao (2009), *Teaching Mathematics in Elementary Schools*, New Delhi: Discovery Publishing House.

Ediger, Marlow, and D. Bhaskara Rao (2011), *Essays on Teaching Mathematics*. New Delhi, India: Discovery Publishing House Pvt. Ltd.

15

Concerns in Teaching Mathematics

There are numerous concerns in the teaching of mathematics. These need to be compared, analyzed, and studied indepth. Changes in the curriculum accrue and they need to be incorporated, if assessed thoroughly. Generally, modification is a key word when thinking of changes to be made of the present in progressing toward a recommended status in mathematics instruction. Changes may be noted from the past in moving toward the present in historical context:

- rote learning and memorization of basic addition, subtraction, multiplication, division facts, in Colonial schools during the seventeenth century
- object lessons in using concrete materials emphasized by Johann Friedrich Pestalozzi (1746-1827). For example, objects were utilized to show meaningfully what five objects and four objects represent in addition
- "gifts" stressed by Friedrich Froebel (1752-1852) which advocated and utilized models of geometric figures such as cubes, rectangular solids, lines, points, planes, cones, and pyramids, in teaching and learning situations. Froebel considered the sphere as an ideal since it had no edges. He used mathematical ideas in his writings in teaching kindergarten children.
- lesson plans proposed by Johann Herbart (1776-1841) and used by his laboratory teachers in training. His steps of teaching included preparation (review and

providing background information to pupils), presentation (teaching the new subject matter in the ensuing lesson), association (relating the two previous steps in teaching so that content does not remain in isolation), generalization (related ideas gained for a conclusion), and use (information achieved is put to use in school and in society).

In noticing the progress made in teaching by Pestalozzi, Froebel, and Herbart, each deal with an innovation in ideas. These innovations were considered issues in their respective days. Their recommendations, in part, were considered as additional issues in time and place.

Present Day Concerns in Teaching

Almost continuously, new issues are identified with their pros and cons. These require analysis, synthesis, and assessment. Selected schools have found it to be expensive in adopting new basal textbooks in mathematics and have gone in the direction of developing their own. Reputable mathematics textbooks contain their own scope ands sequence and are used by many teachers. When texts do not meet the perceived needs of teachers, they may wish to expand time and energy in something that meets personal needs of individual learners. Much research and many meetings are necessary to eventually come up with text materials which are agreed upon. This may have much merit if pupils benefit from the ensuing text developed by teachers. Meticulous work, indeed, is needed to develop reputable mathematics materials for teaching.

Second, how much time should be spent on didactic procedures of teaching such as lectures/explanations versus inquiry and discovery methods? There are mathematics teachers who spend considerable time using explanations and lectures, depending upon pupil maturity, in teaching and learning situations. Carefully sequenced explanations are very worthwhile in assisting individual pupils in understanding the "why" of carrying in addition and multiplication, for example. This, too, might well be explained in large group or class as a whole experiences. However, in the latter, care needs to be taken to make certain selected learners attach meaning within these explanations. There may not be adequate opportunities in securing feedback from pupils at the time lectures are given. The mathematics teacher then must be certain that within smaller groups, or individuals working by the self, all can apply what was presented to the class as a whole. If not, then diagnosis of errors made and remediation applied should receive favourable results. Best it is, if the teacher, in a small group or individually, assists pupils to attach meaning to and provides the necessary response.

Toward the other end of the continuum, the teacher provides ample opportunities for pupils to learn inductively. Thus, teachers need to raise questions which lead pupils to achieve content by discovery. Scaffolding, too, needs to be utilized whereby the learner responds to sequential questions of the teacher which then leads to the appropriate answer. With inductive procedures utilized in mathematics instruction, the learner, also, is the focal point of instruction and comes up with knowledge and skills from within, rather than subject matter coming from the teacher to the child. Within a committee setting, learners may collaborate on finding solutions to problems on their own. The teacher assists when "blind spots" are encountered. Vygotsky (1933 and 1978) strongly advocated small group work for pupils since learning involves a social situation whereby ideas "bounce off their minds," and benefit others. The writer when supervising university student teachers in the public schools found that collaborative work in arithmetic energizes pupils and makes learning exciting. Pupils, then, might challenge each other in a wholesome way in coming up with solutions to problems.

Third, using rewards in teaching has been a somewhat long-term issue. If pupils achieve a specific objective, should they be rewarded with an inexpensive prize? Reinforcement theory emphasizes that a reward needs to be announced prior to the learning activity so that pupils are willing to achieve in order to receive the prize. Advocates of reinforcement theory state that the promise of rewards may be omitted once the learner has been successful in learning over a selected period of time. The reward is directly related to pupil success in goal attainment. Extrinsic motivation has been used to describe reinforcement theory since there is an outside source to motivate achievement.

Toward the other end of the continuum, there are educators who advocate intrinsic motivation in that, from within, the learner has a desire to learn and prizes are not needed to encourage learning. Learning then is its own reward with challenging and interesting2 experiences. Both extrinsic and intrinsic advocates of pupil learning would agree that intermittent praise given judiciously provides feedback to pupils in ongoing achievement and progress.

Fourth, mentoring is a poignant concept to emphasize. Mentors assist beginning teachers in feeling comfortable with knowledge and skills in implementing instruction. Teacher turnover may be minimized with mentors who work well with teachers and can assist newcomers in developing confidence in teaching, as well as helping learners to become higher achievers. Mentors might also assist established mathematics teachers in designing the mathematics curriculum to improve instruction. Teachers also may receive assistance in helping with discipline problems which disrupt the classroom and hinder progress. The mentor is there to guide, assist, and help with instructional problems.

Toward the other end of the continuum, the beginning teacher leans upon his/her own professional training, thinking and ideas to provide for individual differences among pupils in the classroom. The beginning mathematics teacher may consult with an experienced colleague when the need arises pertaining to a problem in instruction.

Fifth, a professional library dealing with mathematics instruction, needs to be in the school setting. Here, the teacher may read journal articles and from basal university textbooks on the latest trends in mathematics teaching. There should be opportunities to discuss with other professionals content encountered, as inservice education. There should be a plethora of other inservice education programmes such as workshops, faculty meetings, as well as attending professional meetings dealing with mathematics instruction.

Toward the other end of the continuum, a mathematics teacher may take the lead in encouraging an inservice education project. The writer's wife, a first grade teacher, asked primary grade teachers to meet on a certain date to discuss what each was doing in teaching mathematics innovatively. She reported a lively discussion and the group made plans to meet again. Successive meetings were held with teachers reporting on trying out new ideas in teaching and the perceived results of each plan. Mathematics teachers might well develop and carry out worthwhile inservice education plans. Teacher development and leadership roles here is to be encouraged. Teacher planned inservice education may be compared to less effective plans which have been determined by those not in face to face connections with classroom learners. What is elaborated upon in the inservice education programmes may be tried out in the local classroom with feedback going back to participants. Ideas for teaching must be evaluated thoroughly prior to, during, and after the trial period. Individual differences must be provided for so that the talents/abilities of each pupil are provided and utilized (Ediger and Rao, 2012).

In Conclusion

The psychology of learning is poignant to emphasize in teaching mathematics. Thus, leanings for pupils must be:

- based on previous mathematical experiences in order to provide quality sequence.
- understandable so that learners attach meaning in each daily lesson and ongoing unit of study.
- interesting so that active involvement is promoted.

- purposeful in order to assist in developing acceptable reasons for full participation in achievement.
- relevant for learners to perceive importance in attaining objectives of instruction.

REFERENCES

Ediger, Marlow, and D. Baskara Rao (2012), *Essays on Teaching Mathematics*. New Delhi, India: Discovery Publishing House Pvt. Ltd.

Vygotsky, Lev (1933 and 1978), *Mind in Society*. Cambridge, Massachusetts: Harvard University Press.

16
Issues in Teaching Mathematics

There are selected issues in mathematics instruction which educators should be well aware of when planning lessons and units of study. These issues provide a basis for thought and discussion when assisting pupils to attain more optimally. Purposeful studying of issues guides mathematics teachers in emphasizing what is relevant in the curriculum. Which issues appear to be relevant?

Developing a Relevant Mathematics Curriculum

There has been a debate pertaining to indepth teaching versus survey procedures. Thus, the issue pertains to teaching mathematical concepts and generalizations depthwise as compared to covering more topics in mathematics in a similar amount of time, making for a survey procedure. Time in teaching each concept and generalization must be considered in making this decision. The important point here is that adequate time must be given to assist pupils to attach meaning in the ongoing teaching and learning experiences.

Indepth processes are to be favoured; however the scope of the curriculum needs to be considered also. How broad should the scope be in mathematics which then allows pupils to truly understand subject matter. It appears that the scope of the mathematics curriculum will be narrower with indepth teaching, since more time will be necessary to achieve conceptual as well as generalizations in learning. The scope is broadened with survey procedures, but less time available for teaching each vital concept and generalization. Might the two points of view view be harmonized with more effective management practices including minimizing discipline problems in order to keep pupils on task, ways of checking pupil attendance, gathering and returning pupil work in mathematics, as well as utilizing the psychology of learning in teaching.

The psychology of learning stresses the securing and maintaining pupil interest in the ongoing lesson. Much time is wasted when pupils look out the window and concentrate on something else than the the lesson being presented. Materials and methods of instruction need to be utilized which favour attention getting approaches, focusing upon objectives of instruction. Interest is a powerful factor in learning. Thus, concrete objects, semi-concrete materials (pictures, illustrations, video tapes, computers and other related technology), as well as the abstract must become an inherent part of the teaching and learning process in mathematics. Inappropriate selection of materials of instruction hinder pupil achievement. Then too, the methods of instruction need careful attention. Inquiry learning as well as other inductive methods aid learner progress and encourages active involvement of pupils in the curriculum. Problem-solving, also, assists pupils to become motivated learners, especially those problems possessing personal purpose. Verification of answers supplied by pupils need to be emphasized. Thus, pupils provide information on how they engaged in obtaining answers (Ediger, 2013).

Too frequently, standardized test scores are the only measurement device looked at when appraising pupil performance in mathematics. A definite numerical result simplifies what pupils are accomplishing. Teacher observations of learner progress are also relevant. Each day of teaching and learning involving pupil progress is then being evaluated, rather than a single score from a standardized test. Thus, in teacher observation, the following may be assessed:

- pupil perseverance in achieving
- effort put for in completing assignments as well as in doing voluntary work

- attitudes of the learner towards mathematics
- learner self-diagnosis and remediation of daily work
- accuracy in mathematical work completed (Ediger and Rao, 2012).

Results from teacher observation of pupil achievement provides feedback for ensuing learnings and lessons. Feedback to the teacher also accrues when appraising learner performance on a longer period of time. Thus, an evaluation covering several weeks of time gives data not only on how well pupils are doing presently, but also brings to bear prior knowledge and skills retained from earlier units taught. Formative evaluation then informs teaching and learning in mathematics. Evaluation, then, is continuous and ongoing. Data driven instruction is certainly in evidence when precise measurements of achievement are utilized to provide needed information on what should be taught to attain objectives of instruction.

Adequate time must be given to encourage mathematics teachers, meeting together, to analyze pupil results from tests and observations made. Here, teachers may learn from each other to improve instruction. They may, for instance, diagnose common errors made by pupils, and hypothesize how best to assist in remedying with high quality teaching and learning situations. Meaning in the mathematics curriculum is salient in that pupils must be able to explain "why" an operation was performed in a mathematical situation. Rigor needs to be stressed so that each pupil works toward optimal achievement and performs as mathematicians do in their profession.

In the article, "Making Mathematicians," Education Update, April 2013 issue, eight standards for Mathematical Practice are a pedagogical North Star of sorts:

1. Make sense of problems and persevere in solving them.
2. Reason abstractly and quantitatively.
3. Construct viable arguments and critique the resigning of others.
4. Model with mathematics.

5. Use appropriate tools strategically.
6. Attend to precision.
7. Look for and make use of structure.
8. Look for and express regularity in repeated reasoning.

REFERENCES

Ediger, Marlow (2013), "The Psychology of Learning in Teaching Mathematics," *Delta k* (50(1), 20-22.

Ediger, Marlow, and D. Bhaskara Rao (2012), *Essays on Teaching Mathematics*. New Delhi, India: Discovery Publishing House Pvt. Ltd.

17

Diagnosis in Mathematics Curriculum

Mathematics teachers need to diagnose the kinds of errors pupils make in order that improved performance is in evidence. Diagnosis provides feedback to the teacher of pupil daily work as well as from mandated test results. Immediate feedback of learner achievement aids in avoiding practising what is incorrect in mathematics. Collectively, mathematics teachers need to discuss the kinds of errors made and elaborate on how to assist learners in achievement. Within collaboration, teachers analyze, study, and provide suggestions on sequential mathematics learnings for pupils. Sequence emphasizes continual progress in an orderly procedure. Practising what is incorrect is more difficult to correct as compared to providing sequential learnings. This leaves room for pupils individually, or collectively, to ponder over complexities in mathematics, such as in problem solving, and come up with correct answers and solutions (Ediger, and Rao, 2013).

Solving Problems in Diagnosis

Teachers of mathematics need to view errors made by pupils in an objective manner. The "why" query is salient here to ascertain causes. From our observations of university student teachers in the public schools of which we supervise, the following are frequent errors made by pupils:

1. Problems in computation: These learners may not have mastered basic learnings such as addition and subtraction facts. If this is a consistent type of error, pupils need to attach meaning to each, followed by practices such as responding to drill using flash cards. This learning opportunity may be accomplished with a peer. There is purpose involved here once a learner perceives reasons for doing this. The purpose is to master these essential facts and not for the sake of drill. Use can be made of basic facts in problem-solving in school and in society.

2. Sometimes, pupils do not utilize reasoning procedures to secure answers to problems: Reasoning is a common mathematical procedure in determining how to do a problem. Incorrect reasoning must be detected and shown "why." Thus, for instance, 2/4 is equal to 6/12 can be shown with a cut out pizza whereby 2/4 of a circle is congruent to 6/12 of a pizza with one covering the area of the other in area. Multiply the numerator and the denominator by the same number does not change the fractional area size; the area is the same. This may be taught inductively whereby pupils through discovery ascertain the answers or deductively in which the teacher demonstrates clearly and meaningfully why multiplying the numerator and the denominator by the same number does not increase area of the involved fractions with applications made by the learner.

3. Proper comprehension of abstract words is necessary in solving word problems: Reading skills are involved across the curriculum and this is definitely true in mathematics. Sometimes, pupils will skip words they cannot identify or put in place an incorrect word. A few pupils may need to have the word problems read to them orally so that they may engage in the proper mathematical procedures. Context clues should be taught here and modeled by the mathematics teacher. Selected phonic learnings might also be stressed.

4. Vocabulary development in mathematics is lacking: Having its own unique vocabulary, mathematics terms need to be mastered so that proficiency in learning might accrue. Sometimes, simple terms such as minus, plus, sum, difference, are perplexing to young children. Older students may need assistance to understand commutative, associative and distributive properties. Vocabulary terms need to be meaningful and read properly. Understanding what is taught is poignant!

5. Pupils may lack a methodology of securing an answer in problem-solving: Thus, the pupils does not focus upon what is essential to obtain a solution. Thus, learners need to flesh out what is needed from the less essential. Also, it is necessary to follow a proper procedure involving number.

6. Pupils may have a very short attention span: The mathematics teacher needs to observe learners to notice if the subject matter is too complex. Then too, he/she must explain mathematics content in a way in which pupils understand what is taught. Words may be simplified and materials of instruction utilized be more concrete. Thus, for example, an increased use of markers may be emphasized for counting, adding, and subtracting. This is done to increase a hands on approach which is more concrete and with less reliance upon abstract words to increase cognition.

7. Lack of interest in mathematics might be a contributing factor: There are numerous ways to teach and for pupils to achieve an objective. The mathematics teacher needs to observe the kinds of experiences which attract learners so that boredom does not enter into the equation. Learning styles are useful considerations in assisting pupils to connect with ongoing lessons and units of study. The following are some of the alternatives: working by the self-instead of in a small group, emphasis upon learning centers versus textbook methods, pupil determined as compared to a teacher chosen sequence in learning, among others. Meeting needs of pupils is salient!

8. Too much haste in wanting to finish a lesson and then not choosing vital data in problem-solving: Each pupil needs to do careful work which emphasizes close reading and doing. The mathematics teacher needs to demonstrate careful, meticulous work as compared to hasty and sloppy endeavors. Too often, pupils do not perceive personal work as being detrimental due to a "getting over with it" attitude.

9. Vaguely understanding a problem and not bothering to receive teacher assistance as needed: Accurate work is necessary in mathematics and this takes time in doing quality work.

10. Poor quality handwriting to present information in mathematics: It becomes difficult in reading information from selected learners.

REFERENCE

Ediger, Marlow, and D. Bhaskara Rao (2013) *Essays on Teaching Mathematics*. New Delhi, India: Discovery Publishing House Pvt. Ltd.

18

Problem-solving in Mathematics Curriculum

Problem-solving is a vital skill in all of life's endeavors, and the mathematics curriculum certainly can make for tremendous progress in the problem-solving arena. Ideally, problems should come from and be identified by pupils. Each has relevant numerical problems to solve. However, it may be difficult to develop a viable mathematics curriculum from this source alone. They might well become an integral part of lesson and unit teaching. Carefully chosen mathematics textbooks with quality scope and sequence may offer a an indepth programme of instruction, providing that the methods of teaching follow the psychology of learning tenets.

Relevant problems are identified by textbook writers, and practical application must be stressed in each problem. The teacher needs to think of strategies which enhance the concept of practicality so that learners perceive its use in both school and in society. Abstractions then become concrete as well as useful.

Problem-solving stresses thought, deliberation, and effort. This is different than offering memorized answers to addition, multiplication, subtraction, and division facts. Although the facts are committed to memory after meaningful learnings, a slow down in problem-solving will occur if mathematical facts are not available for immediate recall in problem solving.

Philosophy of Instruction in Mathematics

Selected educators stress a basics mathematics curriculum. Thus, there are essential learnings all pupils need to achieve.

Quality standardized tests emphasize that every pupil must attain specific, measurably stated objectives. These tests are developed and constructed by experts in the field. They have been field tested to take out kinks, ultimately resulting in valid and reliable tests. From the results of test taking, pupils receive numerical data such as being on the sixtieth percentile. The results are objective and the same score is obtained if computerized or hand scoring is done accurately. Subjectivity is omitted or minimized in the process since all pupils on a given grade level take the same test with the same time limits in test taking. Subjectivity enters in when considerations for differences among pupils are identified such as talents possessed, interests, purposes, and motivation possessed.

With standardized test results, each pupil is compared with others in percentile ranking. Schools are also compared in test results against each other. Making comparisons is to be a motivating device with attempts made by competitors to move upward in progress (Ediger and Rao, 2012).

Feedback from test results may be quite valuable in that it provides teachers with possible information on what to focus upon in ensuing lessons in mathematics. Remedial work is then possible. Mandated testing is quite popular, with a few dissenters. Disadvantages with mandated standardized testing are the following:

- used for high stakes testing for promotional purposes from one grade level to the next. A single test should not solely determine promotion.
- may be utilized to appraise teaching performance. Too much emphasis or weight then is placed on evaluation of teachers by using standardized tests, omitting/ minimizing daily achievement of pupils.
- utilized excessively as a performance measure of pupil achievement in mathematics. A variety of high quality evaluative procedures must be emphasized.

Standardized tests with high validity and reliability can certainly make their many contributions when used to improve individual achievement in mathematics. Thus for example with item analysis, the teacher may pinpoint what was missed by a pupil and with reteaching and remedial work assist learners to up progress and growth.

During daily work in ongoing lessons and units of study, the mathematics teacher has excellent opportunities to observe specifics of achievement, and provide almost immediate assistance to overcome identified weaknesses. However, the pupil must have ample opportunities too work through a problem. Scaffolding might be utilized here in that the teacher asks questions of the learner, thus leading him/her to the correct answer. In the meantime, the learner is challenged to arrive at a solution inductively.

Learning opportunities need to be motivating so that pupil effort in learning is in evidence. A variety of developmentally appropriate activities will assist in providing needed energy levels for achieving. The following may be utilized to provide a sound pedagogically inductive/deductive procedure of instruction:

* manipulative materials as well as semi-concrete items including illustrations
* models and drawings of salient related ideas
* worksheets elaborating on mathematical ideas emphasized in class
* small group experiences focusing on solving a problem
* class as a whole discussing a relevant problem area
* video games and teacher/pupil made games
* textbook materials and entries.

The above-named asterisked materials need to be utilized sequentially to optimize achievement and goal attainment. Individual differences need to be provided for. Each pupil has unique talents, interests, goals, and purposes; the mathematics curriculum may well provide for these differences with the involvement of conscientious teachers.

Many schools utilize basal textbooks in teaching and learning situations. Carefully selected texts, used in high quality lessons and units of study might well offer activities and experiences which meet pupil needs and assist in college and career readiness goals. Here, mathematics teachers need to be certain that each pupil comprehends printed content in word problems. Comprehension stresses meaning and understanding. Thus, pupils need to be able to identify words for reading fluency to occur. Selected words may cause problems in recognition, and after a lesson has been introduced to stimulate learning, the mathematics teacher may do the following as needed:

- place struggling readers in a small group and read aloud the involved subject matter in a word problem, with learners following along in the their textbook. There must be an atmosphere of respect for these pupils and in no way are they to be ridiculed or put down. This approach emphasizes pupils getting to the heart of solving a word problem and not struggling over word recognition. Then too, a good reader might well read aloud, softly, to a child with reading problems to assist the latter in moving on toward toward problem solving activities in mathematics as well as increasing reading performance.
- have pupils, individually, indicate which words present identification problems. Each may be assisted with a problem solving procedure. He/she might then be asked which word fits in properly with the rest of the words in the sentence or paragraph. This eliminates ridiculous words which definitely do not make sense and emphasizes the utilization of context clues. If this is not adequate, the teacher may ask which sound the first letter of the unidentified word makes. The use of context clues and phonics should be adequate in assisting the learner in word identification. If not, additional letters and related sounds might be stressed by the mathematics teacher.
- construct a word wall in the classroom whereby pupils may look at and review new words encountered to

assist in problem-solving. In supervising university student teachers in the classroom, the writer noticed how pupils look at these words on their own during spare time as well as use them in ongoing lessons involving reading.

- use an electronic reader in which the words may be pronounced aloud as the pupil points to each word read orally. Words to understood in terms of vocabulary development may be highlighted and the definition/meaning given. Each learner might keep a personal record of new words encountered with matching definitions given. Reviewing these words helps in reading mathematical subject matter and increases opportunities for solving word problems. It is good if a pupil does not have to struggle over reading words plus solving a problem. The focus needs to be on what is needed to solve the math problem. However, reading content accurately is indeed salient in mathematics and in all curriculum areas.

As the teacher circulates in the classroom, he/she notices the kinds of difficulties pupils experience in problem-solving. Here, teaching definitely is not telling or lecturing, but to guide pupils to think indepth as to what is needed to arrive at an accurate solution to a problem. The mathematics teacher may model orally the steps needed and "why" to solve a problem. Periodically, pupils also need to explain the processes necessary. In this way, the mathematics teacher may record what is needed in ensuing lessons. Progress should be sequential within the pupil and assistance provided to maximize achievement (Ediger, 2007).

REFERENCES

Ediger, Marlow (2007), "Meaning in Reading Instruction," *Reading Improvement*, 44(4), 217-220.

Ediger, Marlow, and D. Bhaskara Rao (2012), *Essays on Teaching Mathematics*. New Delhi, India: Discovery Publishing House.

19

Psychology in Teaching Mathematics

Emphasizing the psychology of teaching and learning assists in upping achievement. It needs to be stressed in selecting objectives, learning experiences, and appraisal procedures. Thus, the individual pupil is the focal point in ascertaining where each is achieving presently, and this must then take into account the total number of learners in the classroom. International test results have been in the middle for the United States when comparisons among nations are made. However, test results do not tell the entire story since the attitudinal dimension is short changed/omitted in these results.

Certainly, high quality attitudes are relevant in mathematics. They provide motivation for achievement and learning in ongoing lessons and units of study. Stressing the attitudinal/affective dimension in learning is vital for mathematics teachers!

The Affective Input in Achievement

What might the teacher do to develop positive feelings toward mathematics? Pupils differ from each in diverse ways and this needs adequate consideration when providing for individual differences among learners in a classroom; the following are recommended to up quality feelings among learners toward mathematics:

- call pupils by name and show interest in their individual talents, hobbies, and goals in life
- be polite to pupils in all situations and in return encourage politeness to the teacher

- assist pupils, specifically, when needed in problem solving so that progress in the ensuing activity may be made
- have pupils work collaboratively in small groups to arrive at answers and solutions to mathematical problems. Harmonious relationships are to be practised and reinforced
- let pupils work in dyads to remedy deficiencies
- help pupils realize that mistakes made in math can be remedied and provide guidance for continuous achievement in ensuing tasks
- assist pupils to realize that effort, not ability alone is significant in achievement.

The psychology of learning is in evidence when learning activities are changed to meet pupil needs. Thus, for example, concrete objects are utilized for learners in attaching meaning to simple addition, such as three sticks and two sticks are joined together and counted as five sticks. By replacing the abstract 3 + 2 = 5, with the concrete learners can see realistically how the two concrete objects equal five. The abstraction might then be written to show it is directly related to the concrete. If more information is needed by pupils, use of illustrations may follow or be used concurrently with the concrete materials as well as the abstract. These are foundational learnings for pupils and with sequential achievement, pupils might realize ever complex understandings such as 1,269 + 4,326 = 5,595 which would be cumbersome but can be shown with objects, illustrations, and the related abstract form. Thus, pupils need to attach meaning at the earliest learning possible in mathematics so that related, sequential subject matter and skills are also understood. The concrete, semi-concrete (pictorial form and illustrations, as well as the abstract may be interchanged as needed to meet needs of pupils. At any point, diagnosis and remediation might occur; however, learners need to be given ample time to think, analyze, and become increasingly independent in working on solutions in mathematical situations.

Mathematics art is a good way for young children to secure basic learnings in geometry. When supervising university student teachers in the public schools, the writer was interested in kindergarten/first grade pupils actively engaged in naming neatly cut out geometrical figures from different colors of construction paper. The cutouts were located on the teacher's desk and a pupil picked up needed geometrical figures, correctly naming them orally, and then proceeding to the art centre in the classroom. The pieces were pasted together on a single sheet of paper to make a down, house, barn, among other things. The scenes and sights were quite creative as portrayed by these kindergarten children. They were able to name each geometrical figure in the art product. Respect for each other was a further objective being emphasized. Geometry art serves as a building block to more complex, sequential objectives in the arena. Attaching meaning to each geometrical figure leads to the identification of squares, rectangles, among others in the real world such as doors and windows, as well as a circular window on the school building in the out of doors. A word wall containing drawings, labels, and ordered definitions of geometrical learnings brings on interest, enthusiasm, and knowledge for classroom teachings well as for pupil browsing as they walk past ttie word wall. A Kindergarten through high school sequence in geometry must be in the offing.

In teaching fractions, the mathematics teacher might show an attractive pizza, in circular form. The pizza may be divided into congruent fractional parts such as halves, fourths, eighths, depending upon goal objectives being taught. Another pizza may be divided into thirds and sixths. In the first pizza, the teacher may assist pupils to realize inductively/deductively that two halves is equal to one whole. The two halves can be placed over the whole. A prerequisite learning stresses that one ½ means one of two parts being considered. The abstract form may be written directly next to the pizza. Meaningful learning, in sequence, indicates that pupils understand and attach meaning to ongoing experiences and activities. Memorization is definitely not emphasized. When pupils correctly verbalize/demonstrate, accurately, obtained subject matter, mastery then is in evidence (Edsger and Rao, 2012).

Working colaboratively in small pupils in problem-solving. Working harmoniously, learners then pool their information and thinking to arrive at a solution. They need to possess tenacity and grit to problem solve. It is easy to give up in frustration, but rather pupils need to persevere in coming up with an accurate solution. Critical thinking is involved when separating facts from opinions as well as accurate from inaccurate ideas. Learning from mistakes is poignant and should be looked upon in that manner. In collaborative settings, pupils challenge and leam from each other. When they get "stuck," there is a pupil or the teacher to provide a hint on what needs to be done so that progress may be made. Extreme struggling over solving a problem is not recommended, but putting forth much effort to problem solve is a virtue to be rewarded. Creative efforts are to be praised such as in finding a unique algorithm or methodology in an ongoing lesson or unit of study. Telling and lecturing is not teaching, but makes for passivity on the part of pupils. It is the learner who must attain and acquire in active active manner (Ediger, 2012).

Being competent in reasoning is a major component of present day mathematical skills. Reasoning from evidence aids in problem-solving. Perseverance is needed here in putting forth much energy in school work. Motivation provides for higher energy levels and stimulating activities and are essential. Turning off in objectives achievement invites low progress as well as interest. Learning opportunities must be chosen on the basis of being practical, stimulating, and motivational. The leaner must reach out and engage in then activities which promote achievement.

Teachers need to develop feelings of resilience within pupils whereby feelings and attitudes of defeat as well as not trying are negative options to problem-solving. Rather bouncing back from failure is emphasized, and with good teaching, each pupil may experience success. The zone of proximal development (ZPD) indicates an area in which achievement is challenging and possible. Beyond the zone of proximal development, the teacher may scaffold learner progress to even higher reasonable levels of achievement. Thus, through encouragement as well as sequenced appropriate learnings, pupils might well attain as optimally as possible. Teachers need to study and implement tenets of ZPD. Inservice education, focusing on ZPD, needs indepth study and practising tenets therein in the reguiar classroom. Definite to be need scheduling which meet up with the objectives, followed by actually trying ZPD psychology in as well as to the pertaining to what transpired (See Vygotsky, 1978).

Evaluation is highly salient here in that analyzing results might pinpoint significant findings in improving mathematics instruction. Growth in instructional knowledge/skills is a further achievement in committee endeavors.

Mathematics teachers must be confident in teaching a wide range of learners. Thus, the gifted, talented, average, slow learners, mentally deficient, among other classification of pupils need to achieve as optimally as possible. The usefulness of math, not only in school, but also in society must ever be emphasized. Pupils need to have ample opportunities to discuss how they have utilized mathematical content in everyday situations, thus assisting peers in ciass to see its prevailing values.

Appraising Pupil Achievement and Progress

The mathematics teacher needs to be skilful in observing achievement in everyday work that pupils do in ongoing lessons. Continuous and sequential appraisal is highly important. The teacher might then notice the kinds of errors made by pupils and offer remediation. Meaning and understanding by pupils must be attached to concepts and generalizations being stressed in ensuing learning opportunities. Too frequently, school administrators and teachers pay careful attention to mandated/standardized test results largely. They are important, however assessing carefully the everyday school work, also, is highly significant. Assisting pupils each day to experience quality sequence might well help to up test sores in mandated/standardized tests given annually.

Then too, data on annual tests need to be studied carefully. What is it that pupils are lacking? With item analysis, specifics can be noted and these provide feedback for instruction. Mathematics teachers then need to look beyond the percentile for a learner, but think about meeting pupil needs to be successful in mathematics use. Standardized tests need to be studied indepth to notice how validity was determined as well as reliability. Both concepts are very important when analyzing the of standardized tests. With validity, the question arises, "Does the test truly measure achievement in what has been/should be taught in mathematics?" Pertaining to reliability, the poignant question is. "Does the test measure consistently?" This takes time and effort to determine the validity and reliability of each standardized test being considered or used.

Humaneness in Mathematics Lessons and Units of Study

Social and emotional learning (SEL) are important considerations in curriculum development. Social learning is emphasized whenever pupils work together to solve problems in mathematics. Harmony among members makes for a pleasant learning environment. No one likes to work in a rude, hostile environment. The teacher is a guide in modelling and assisting learners to cooperate for the common good by utilizing talents in the ongoing activity.

Emotional learning takes place when feelings are positive toward the task and toward peers, as well as toward the teacher. Negative attitudes hinder achievement and progress. They also make time and effort unpleasant within mathematical experiences.

REFERENCES

Ediger, Marlow (2012), "Toward a High Quality Mathematics Curriculum," *Experiments in Education*, 40(4), 45-57.

Ediger, Marlow and D. Bhaskara Rao (2012), *Essays on Teaching Mathematics*, New Delhi, India: Discovery Publishing House.

Vygotsky, Len (1978), Mind in Society, *The Development of Higher Mental Processes*. Cambridge, Massachusetts: Harvard University Press.

20

The Mathematics Curriculum and the Psychology of Learning

To become increasingly efficient in teaching mathematics the teacher needs to utilize major principles of learning from psychology. Self-efficacy is a major goal of all teachers in that they feel comfortable in a variety of mathematical teaching situations. This involves teaching the mentally impaired, the physically handicapped, visually and hearing impaired, as wells talented and gifted learners, among others. Self-efficacy is developed through being properly certified to teach mathematics as well as :

- studying and reading content on teaching and learning
- taking graduate course work from an accredited university
- participating actively in ongoing inservice education programmes offered by the involved school
- discussing with colleagues ways of improving mathematics instruction
- doing an independent study on problems in teaching mathematics.

With adequate background information on mathematics as well as teaching pedagogy, the teacher is able to work effectively with any classification of pupils in the classroom setting (Ediger and Rao, 2012).

The Competent Mathematics Teacher

Knowledgeable teachers are skilful in stressing indepth teaching. He/she is able to provide needed explanations to correct pupil inaccurate conceptions. Accuracy is a key goal of instruction and pupils need proper assistance in doing mathematics with meaning and understanding. Thus, the learner is able to provide precise explanations why a certain problem was completed in the way he/she gave. Here, the teacher provides guidance, where necessary, to pupils in doing processes and procedures correctly. This is a major goal for teachers to possess much subject matter in the instructional arena. At the same time vital pedagogical procedures must be in the offing to assist pupils in developmental and remedial mathematics.

Direct teaching involving clear explanations are necessary so that pupils might understand content in sequence. Thus, the explaining part provides information for the pupil to move forward. At other times, inquiry learning becomes salient. For the individual pupil, this might emphasize the teacher asking questions in sequence which aids the learner in coming up with the correct answer. Then too, inquiry learning is important in teaching small groups or the class as a whole. The concept of "scaffolding" also becomes important here. The mathematics teacher guides a brief questioning period in helping pupils use previously acquired knowledge to come up with a needed solution or answer. Critical thinking is in evidence when pupils are assisted to sort the vital from the unimportant in problem solving. The creative element, also, is inherent when pupils come up with a new solution or algorithm to a problematic situation. Knowledge of pedagogy is salient here. Involving pupil responses is important since it provides ownership of the curriculum to the learner as well as listening to these responses to ascertain the mathematical developmental level of each learner (Ediger, 2011).

Indirect teaching and learning stresses the importance of increased learner input in ongoing experiences. The focal point in achieving is the pupils who must master mathematical content. The teacher sets the stage for attaining of objectives of instruction. Inquiry learning is also emphasized here, with the pupil constructing sequence, in degrees, but the mathematics teacher remains as relevant as ever since he/she must be able to raises vital questions which motivate learners.

The pupil moves forward in progress with teacher encouragement and pupil effort. Indirect instruction inspires learners since stimulating questions are raised as needed with related responses coming from pupils individually. Sequence increasingly resides within the pupil as he/she builds on previously presented ideas. As seamlessly as possible, pupil ordering of learning is promoted by the mathematics teacher and yet pupils see ensuing consequences of attainment.

Learning styles need to be stressed in that preferred means of achievement might be individual, committee/collective endeavors, or a combination of both. With individual work and assignments, each pupil is responsible for object achievement. The pupil needs to signal with raised hand, or with signs of frustration, if help is necessary at a given point. Prior to this time, the mathematics teacher has assisted in providing background experiences for learners in the classroom setting. Still, a learner may face difficulties in word problems or in computation. With collective endeavors, pupils have also experienced background information with the class as a whole, but now it it is up to the group to problem solve. Ideas within the group must be respected and each needs to participate actively in the ongoing activity. Mathematics problem-solving is the objective, here, of collaborative work with problems such as the following:

- finding the area in square units of carpet to be installed in the classroom
- solving an equation with one unknown
- factoring and finding the least common denominator or greatest common factor.

In reality, pupils need to become proficient in both individual and collaborative endeavors since in society the individual engages in each. Balance between the two needs adequate emphasis.

Innovations and technology must be brought in to the curriculum. Pupils need to become proficient in their use. Pupils from lower income level homes may lack in opportunities to work with computers, and the school must provide needed opportunities for pupils to become skilled with technology utilization. Otherwise, individuals are left out of becoming employable in many situations later at the work place. Teachers need to emphasize the following criteria when using technology in the mathematics curriculum:

- knowledge and skills must be on the developmental level of the learner.
- surveys should be made of the present achievement level of each pupil.
- ensuing learnings must be based on the present level of attainment.
- sequential skills and content may then be taught, with encouragement given pupils to achieve at higher levels of accomplishment.
- scaffolding objectives guide pupils to do well in technology utilization.

Competent mathematics teachers know when and where the use of technology may help pupils master salient learnings. Uses of technology are not for the sake of doing so, but to assist pupils in achievement.

Emotional intelligence (EI) is important for teachers, as well as learners, in that feelings are involved in teaching and learning situations. Thus, the mathematics teacher, for example, must realize that patience is salient in working with pupils to attain optimally. At the same time, the teacher must have reasonable, high expectations for each learner. The cognitive domain is at work in that relevant subject matter is being taught and learned, as well the affective dimension with its focus on the feeling dimension. Thus, appropriate feelings need to be in evidence, along with cognition (Ediger, 2012).

REFERENCES

Ediger, Marlow (2011), "Assessing Pupil Achievement in Mathematics," *Journal of Instructional Psychology*.

Ediger, Marlow (2012), ''Teaching Mathematics and Emotional Intelligence," *Experiments in Education*, 40(1), 27-30.

Ediger, Marlow, and D. Bhaskara Rao (2012), *Essays on Teaching Mathematics*. New Delhi, India: Discovery Publishing House.

21

Balance in Mathematics Curriculum

There are selected issues in teaching mathematics which indicate a need for research, study, and revision in thinking, if needed. These issues reflect a necessity in providing the best curriculum possible to meet individual needs. Pupils possess different needs due to abilities, interests, and learning styles.

Viewing Different Approaches and Procedures

How much time should b allotted to pupils working collaboratively as compared to individual or class as a whole experiences? There are mathematics teachers who strongly emphasize collaborative endeavors in teaching and learning situations. Thus, learners work in small groups to do an assignment or enrichment activity. Individuals in society work in groups, generally, in the work force. It is salient to get along well with others in the societal arenas. Vygotsky (1933 and 1978) stressed the importance of collaborative endeavors since education is a social endeavor. Within a small group, then, ideas "bounce" off the minds of individuals toward others. Thus, learning involves people interacting in securing ideas. Toward the other end of the continuum, selected pupils achieve best working by the self. This, also, might be considered a style of learning. The mathematics teacher must study pupils to notice under which conditions they do best, individually as compared to collaboratively. No doubt, some kind of rational balance needs to be in evidence between the two.

Second, there are mathematics teachers who lecture much in teaching and learning situations. There are times, of course, whereby pupils need clear explanations in a given mathematical problem. The teacher must be knowledgeable to impart this information in an effective manner. The content comes from the teacher and is adjusted to the achievement level of the learner(s). Politeness and ample consideration for the affective dimension must be inherent in all teaching and learning situations.

Somewhat opposite of lecture/explanation methods of instruction, the mathematics teacher might use inductive procedures whereby, he/she asks sequential questions of the learner which then leads to the correct answer. The responses then come from within or from the pupil. In supervising university student teachers in the public schools, the writer always enjoyed observing pupils make discoveries.

Third, selected teachers teach mathematics as a possible chore for pupils to be endure, even though meaning is emphasized. They believe in academic subject matter being rather unpleasant to learn, but like in daily life, the pleasant as well as the unpleasant tasks need adequate attention. There are parents who agree with this school of thought. William Chandler Bagley (1874-1946), a leading educator in his day, believed strongly in pupils learning the academics in a disciplined manner. Mathematics was to be taught as separate subject, not as integrated content. Reducing or eliminating these boundaries weakened any academic discipline such as mathematics. Bagley, also, opposed activity centered curricula including the project method, which is rather commonly emphasized in mathematics lessons and units. Within a project, there can be considerable measurement in its completion. Here, a practical use is made of abstract mathematical learnings. Application of previous learnings is being stressed.

Somewhat opposite in philosophy of teaching is that the abstract should be made highly concrete for it to be relevant as well as interesting. Thus, in teaching mathematics on the early primary grade levels for example, pupils:

- count the number of individuals who will eat lunch in school, as well as later in the day count who will be drinking milk in the afternoon
- record the number of absences in sequential school days
- make a chart showing temperature readings on an outdoor thermometer
- design a block length of stores in a city, using empty cereal boxes
- do a mural of a farm scene; much mathematics is utilized here in securing dimensions.

In each of the above-named activities, pupils do participate in reading and writing experiences which are integrated into the curriculum.

Fourth, inservice experiences for teachers may be planned for and implemented, largely by supervisors and administrators. These experiences should provide for needs of learners in providing for individual differences. Ways of meeting these needs in terms of stated objectives, learning activities to attain each, as well as evaluation procedures, valid and reliable, which assess pupil achievement, are developed and designed.

Toward the other end of the continuum, mathematics teachers are heavily involved in planning, devising, as well as implementing the inservice programme. Teachers, here, lean upon their own professional experiences in teaching pupils when planning inservice education. Teachers may then try out agreed upon ideas when teaching pupils in the classroom. The results might well be reported back to inservice education participants. A teacher centered as compared to a supervisor/administrator plan of inservice education needs to be studied and ascertain which meets needs of teachers and pupils most in assisting the latter to achieve more optimally in mathematics. The two plans may also be blended in making for quality in assisting teachers to achieve well in teaching and learning situations (Ediger and Rao, 2009).

In closing

Many changes are occurring in the teaching of mathematics. It behoves the teacher to stay abreast of these changes to assist optimal learner progress. Technology use needs to be increased, not for the sake of doing so, but to provide for individual differences in each classroom. Then too, teachers need to pursue university courses from an accredited university which ultimate leads to a graduate degree in mathematics education. Here, a balanced program of mathematical content and methods of instruction is recommended.

REFERENCES

Ediger, Marlow, and D. Baskara Rao (2009), *School Science Education.* New Delhi, India: Discovery Publishing House.

Vygotsky, Len (1933 and 1978), *Mind in Society.* Cambridge, Massachusetts: Harvard University Press.

22
Selection of Mathematics Textbooks

The utilization of textbooks in mathematics has a rather long history. They have been revised numerous times; perhaps, one of the greatest revisions came in 1957 following the Soviet Union's successful launching of Sputnik into space. Fearing that the Soviet Union was more successful in space exploration and in military endeavors, the Unites States successfully sent up their own space object in 1958. What was important here, from the standpoint of mathematics instruction in the United States was the amount of moneys Congress appropriated in improving public school instruction in mathematics and science. There were several heavily funded groups to develop what were then titled "Modern School Mathematics." Groups such as the Greater Cleveland Mathematics Project, The Madison Project, The School Mathematics Study Group, and the University of Illinois Arithmetic Project were comprised of leading mathematicians at colleges and universities who developed new and innovative mathematics curricula (Ediger and Rao, 2012).

Mathematics and science teachers attended approved universities for course work, paid for their by NDEA moneys, which included stipends for spouses and offspring for food and living quarters.

The above-named study groups provided content for well-known publishing companies which printed new editions of modern school mathematics, including Scott Foresman in 1959, revised in 1961, to incorporate further new research and recommendations. Few remember these study groups and what was recommended. The structure of knowledge, inductive learning, and specific, precise terminology, are remnants of the then modern school mathematics.

Use of Basal Textbooks

Basals chosen by mathematics teachers in a school are written by well-known mathematicians and curriculum specialists. They are published by leading textbook publishers with an annotations and/or accompanying manual. The text, when followed contains learning experiences in mathematics which are varied. The mathematics teacher can bring in additional activities as perceived necessary. He/she may use the text as a guide or follow it religiously when teaching pupils. The methods procedures listed might also be modified from didactic procedures to inquiry methods. This should be adjusted according to pupil needs. The manual provides suggestions for objectives, learning activities, as well as appraisal procedure. In supervising university student teachers in the public schools, the writer found that student/regular teachers utilized didactic procedures somewhat heavily and followed the adopted textbook faithfully. There were always exceptions with teachers utilizing the basal as a guide, by bringing in new ideas into teaching and learning situations.

Following the basal textbook carefully in a sequential manner might make for good teaching if:

- the ensuing content is based upon previously acquired concepts and generalizations.
- quality scope and sequence for each grade level is evaluated which is a part of the order of contents, covered in the text.
- enthusiasm for mathematics continues to be fostered and encouraged.
- motivation for learning accrues through various learning experiences.

Mathematics instruction must focus upon the pupil. The learner is the one who is to achieve objectives of instruction.

These new, recommended objectives represent pre-school through high school, preparing the learner for college or career as the ensuing years progress. Teachers who are well versed in academic subject matter are able to assist pupils in daily work when diagnosing errors and remediation. Indepth learning is salient in order that each learner truly understands what is involved in mathematical operations. Shallow, survey approaches in "covering much ground" need to be substituted with intensified meaning procedures of instruction. Poignant ideas, not trivia, must be inherent in teaching and learning situations. Too much time has been wasted in trying to hurry learning when readiness is not there to acquire new subject matter.

Those public schools who feel that the common core objectives need implementing have, in selected public schools, shelved textbook use for developing their own mathematics curriculum. This is indeed a complex task which makes for hours and hours of devoted work by teachers and supervisors in coming up with a new math curriculum. A plethora of reference sources, emphasizing mathematics instruction need perusal. Ideas from experienced math teachers also are highly salient to consider. There are vital questions and problems to consider here, including the following:

- Will this amount to "reinventing the wheel" since volumes of subject matter are in the offing for consideration?
- Will this take an excess amount of teacher time in developing the new curriculum?
- Might revising subject matter content of a highly recommended basal series be a better approach?
- Will there be agreement, of committee members, on what is vital in mathematics instruction?
- Are there other facets of math teaching which committee members should rather focus upon, such as increased use of technology?

Teaching of mathematics involves both high quality academic subject matter and pedagogy. Psychological tenets in teaching mathematics must strongly emphasize the following:

- pupils need to be heavily involved in each lesson and unit of study with fascinating learning experiences. Attention to the task at hand assists in achieving good sequence in achievement. Each lesson must be based on previous experiences.
- pupils need to be tenacious and understand textbook content. Subject matter is not there for rote learning and memorization but rather to secure meaningful ideas, mathematical content must assist learners to attach meaning to each new process, be it regrouping and renaming in addition and subtraction, commutative and associative principles in addition and multiplication, among others.
- pupils need to experience poignant ideas, relevant in today's society, not the trivial and not the unimportant. Mathematics teachers need to stay abreast with the latest in subject matter and pedagogy.
- pupils must use what has been acquired so that it is not forgotten nor becomes hazy in the minds of pupils. With utilization, mathematical content becomes practical and utilitarian. The writer enjoys studying mathematics for its own sake, as a retired professor of education. However, public school pupils may not develop these feelings in achieving mathematical ideas for their sake. They are young and must first build up a repertoire of facts, concepts, and generalizations, relevant in any situation.
- pupils need guidance to perceive purpose in an ensuing process and product content being studied in mathematics. This helps learners in feeling energized in the classroom setting. Reasons then accrue for achieving objectives. Purpose exists for pupils achieving indepth knowledge and skills in fundamental ideas in mathematics.

- pupils must learn to appraise the self as well as the teacher evaluating evaluating learner progress. Both need to be heavily involved here. A conscientious learner assesses his/her own work each day. With careful work and knowledgeable background information gleaned from previous learnings, the pupil becomes self-efficacious in doing mathematical operations and looks forward to becoming increasingly self-sufficient in the mathematics curriculum. Feedback is utilized from completed school work to improve future attempts. The teacher's role is to help pupils understand and apply subject matter in an ensuing context. Too many pupils fall by the wayside in teaching and learning situations. What is lost out on must be remediated. Life in school and in the societal realm emphasizes each person being responsible for mastering necessary mathematical content in daily transactions.

In Conclusion

Mathematics textbooks, carefully selected, are tools to use in implementing a quality curriculum and should be used flexibly to assist each pupil to achieve more optimally. Teacher developed mathematics programmes which might replace the basal text also need to provide for individual differences among learners. There must be agreement, here, on these two statements. Whether on the daily level or on standardized tests, used to measured to measure learner progress, feedback must be used to improve learnings in ensuing lessons. Formative assessments are good to utilize in noticing where a pupil is in achievement at midpoints within ongoing units of study. The mathematics teacher wants to know how well pupils are doing daily, within and at the end of each mathematics unit of study. The results provide data and information on learner progress (Ediger and Rao, 2013). Each teacher must keep abreast of the latest innovation in teaching and learning situations including I Pads, as well as blended learning—versus traditional, among others.

REFERENCES

Ediger, Marlow, and D. Bhaskara Rao (2012), *Essays on Teaching School Mathematics*. New Delhi, India: Discovery Publishing House.

Ediger, Marlow, and D. Bhaskara Rao (2013), *Curriculum and School Teacher*. New Delhi, India: Discovery Publishing House Pvt. Ltd.

23

Assurance of Quality in Mathematics Instruction

High quality mathematics instruction is needed for each pupil in the school setting. There are criticisms in society of not narrowing the gap in mathematics achievement between the races. The mathematics teacher must do the best possible to assist each learner to attain as much as possible. Pupils differ from each other in a plethora of ways, including interest, achievement, and perceiving purpose in mathematics. The mathematics curriculum must help each learner to be ready for college/the work place after high school graduation. Expectation for learners is higher than ever when listening to reports of PISA, NAESP, and state mandated test results. Whether this should be the major procedure of ascertaining quality in the curriculum is up for debate. Are there additional ways of determining how successful pupils are in mathematics, other than through testing methodology? Might there be pupils who do well in mathematics in practical situations, such as using mathematics in building different structures? To develop a quality curriculum, adequate financing is necessary such as purchasing computers and other technology, as well as reputable textbooks, among others.

Developing Quality in Mathematics Instruction

The mathematics teacher must possess a philosophy of providing for individual differences. This means that each learner needs to achieve as well as possible regardless of ability and talent levels. Then too, pupils need to like mathematics as a subject matter area. The mathematics teacher must guide pupils to concentrate on mathematics and not on something else during instructional time. Learning experiences need to be:

* stimulating and of interest to pupils
* reasonable for learners to be successful
* useful and relevant in ongoing experiences
* accepted by pupils as possessing reason for their inclusion
* engaging in all aspects of their implementation (Ediger and Rao, 2012).

To be successful, mathematics teachers need to incorporate the above asterisked items as the psychology of instruction. However, there are additional criteria to emphasize for self-efficacy feelings on the part of the teacher.

Indepth teaching of mathematics is highly important. Too frequently, shallow covering of objectives in ongoing units of study has been in vogue. However, to truly understand content, pupils need subject matter understandings whereby they are able to explain why a certain procedure was utilized in problem-solving. This provides feedback to the teacher if meaning has been attached to ongoing experiences. Indepth teaching has made it so that the learner can provide a thorough understanding of a given process in mathematics. Role learning and memorization will not suffice since this indicates survey approaches.

Then too, pupils need to use verification in explaining the why of performing an operation of solving a problem. Mathematical reasoning is salient such as why the commutative, associative, and distributive properties work in certain situations, but not in others. Accuracy is a key concept in mathematics. Hastily done work in a slovenly manner is opposite of doing satisfactory work in mathematics. The pupil must develop habits of being meticulous, disciplined, as well as mannerly in completing requirements, accurately, as well as neatly done.

The school/classroom environment is a significant factor in teaching and learning situations. Too frequently, content acquisition becomes the major element in planning the curriculum. There are a plethora of other factors which enter into the equation. Distractions hinder environmental factors. These include discipline problems and an inadequate setting arrangements of pupils. Pupils must experience a teaming environment which fosters achievement as well as positive attitudes toward mathematics. Then too respect for and among pupils as well as respect for the classroom teacher are salient. It behooves each school to evaluate the quality of the environment for pupil learning, and, if necessary, conduct inservice education opportunities to minimize negative factors. There are occasions, then, whereby higher levels of cognition might be stressed including critical and creative thinking. Indepth teaching emphasizes securing pupil attention to truly have instruction looking at the why of a mathematical operation. The concept of analysis becomes important here. This, also, might well emphasize opportunities for review in a spiral curriculum. To prevent ideas from becoming vague or hazy, interesting review activities need to be in the offing. The need of the child must be the focal point. What is it that the learner needs to be successful in when emphasizing sequential leanings? Success is a powerful motivator in moving forward when making progress in ongoing activities and experiences. Ensuing subject matter must always make sense to the learner. Subject matter and skills must meet up with the needs of the learner.

Reading of word problems might become a problem to pupils even though they understand the necessary computations. Mathematics teachers then need to become teachers of reading so that pupils can make sense of content read. Stumbling over unknown words and making wrong guesses as to what is needed in problem solving are indeed frustrating to pupils. It is essential then that proper guidance be given in the recognition and identification of the unknown. The teacher may assist through several helpful approaches in correctly-identifying words. The use of context clues, probably, is a first procedure which needs to be utilized. Thus, the pupil makes an educated guess on the word not recognized by providing a word which makes sense with the other words in the sentence, or even paragraph. To give ridiculous words wastes time and energy. Always ask the learner if the word supplied for the unknown is meaningful. Very quickly, the pupils will narrow down the provided words to that which make sense. If not, have the pupil view the first letter of the unknown and sound it out. This procedure truly narrows down to what is correct. There are selected first letter consonants in unknown words which are very consistent between symbol and sound. Applied phonics has much merit in their teaching and does help in recognizing the unknown. Unknown words may be printed neatly on a mathematics word wall for pupil future reference.

When supervising university student teachers in the public schools, the writer has been amazed at the number of learners in their spare time who study these words. This does aid pupils in supplying correct words for that which might well be the unknown in reading (Ediger, 2012).

Social development is important, and the mathematics curriculum can certainly be of help in this area. For instance, committee and collaborative learning experiences might well assist pupils in getting along well with others, providing there is adequate direction from the teacher. Thus, the mathematics teacher needs to place pupils within committees which will further, not hinder, social achievement. The writer has observed collaborative endeavors which are actually harmful to children. There needs to be established rules for learners to abide by. These rules are clearly stated and enforced. The following are quality rules for committee work and their evaluation:

- rudeness is not permitted and ideas presented within a committee must be respected
- each participant must be actively involved and not be passive with nothing to contribute
- achievements from a committee need to be shared with other pupils in the classroom.

Problem-solving collaboratively is challenging to many in small group endeavors. Thus, a word problem, properly introduced by the mathematics teacher, might well fascinate many learners. There certainly can be much interaction among members in working toward problem solutions. Good attitudes toward committee members should be very valuable in assisting pupils to grow in doing well socially. Members on a committee may be changed so that interacting among participants of varied personalities is possible.

Communicating with parents is important! There are a plethora of methods and means of communication such as e-mais, telephone, mobile devices, along with parent/teacher face to face, among others. The point being to improve mathematical learnings for pupils. Discuss specific problems which pupils face and how parents may assist as in:

- computations involving the four major operations
- working with fractions such as reducing to lowest terms, determining the least common multiple (LCM); the greatest common factor (GCF); addition, subtraction, multiplication, and division of fractions; and understanding the inverse operation in division of fractions regrouping and renaming in the four basic processes.

Manipulative devices should be utilized in understanding diverse mathematics. Communication with parents should be:

- relaxing and free of negative anxiety
- open ended with freedom to identify problems and working toward solutions

- positive in treating others with respect involving the teacher and the parent
- evaluative with parents and the teacher cooperatively looking at test results as well as daily work of the pupil.

REFERENCES

Ediger, Marlow (2012), "Psychology of Learning in Teaching Mathematics," *Delta K*, 50(1), 20-21.

Ediger, Marlow, and D. Bhaskara Rao (2012), *Essays on Teaching Mathematics*. New Delhi, India, Discovery Publishing House Pvt. Ltd.

24

Factors that Assist Mathematics Achievement

There are selected factors which might well help pupil achievement in mathematics. These need to be studied, and analyzed and conclusions realized. Public schools need to possess a special place where quality video tapes, teaching mathematics journals and university level mathematics education textbooks, internet, and web sources are available to acquire relevant knowledge and skills to use in ongoing units of study in the classroom. The psychology of learning, among other factors, must be stressed in teaching and learning situations in order to optimize achievement and progress in mathematics. Thus, pupils need to connect subject to the self, to experiences in society, and to the school setting.

Class Size and Learner Progress

How might a class be organized so that pupils may benefit from instruction? This appears to be a perennial question. Hopefully, class size will not exceed, approximately, 20-25 pupils. This should make it possible to teach all pupils effectively.

Pupils may be taught in large group instruction. To initiate a new mathematical unit of study, the teacher must use teaching materials which are clearly visible to all in the classroom. Needed materials of teaching may include a large place value chart with paper strips to show ones, tens, hundreds, and thousands values, as well as congruent objects to be used as markers indicating place value. The mathematics teacher may then demonstrate to pupils how to regroup and rename in addition and subtraction. He/she observes pupils carefully to notice that each is listening carefully and quality learning is in evidence. The learnings are paced and sequential so that learners individually have opportunities to acquire facts, concepts, and generalizations necessary to perform these operations successfully. The mathematics teacher observes pupils carefully to notice engagement as each attends, watches, and notices poignant learnings.

Next, the teacher divides pupils into groups of four. These may be heterogeneous or homogeneous depending upon the purpose involved. Each set of four receives a sheet of problems and a smaller place value chart to practice the objectives emphasized in the larger group. The teacher circulates among the committees to notice time on task behaviours as well as meanings pupils attach to place value. Interests of pupils is noticed within each small group and the quality of interactions is also observed. The teacher then carefully monitors achievement to notice what pupils do not understand with assistance given as needed to overcome problem areas. However, it is good to have pupils ponder and discuss indepth necessary ideas in regrouping and renaming. Selected pupils learn best in social situations whereby ideas circulate within a small group of learners.The mathematics teacher records and dates problem areas as well as progress made by pupils using anecdotal approaches.

Cooperative teaching may also be used whereby involved teachers work together to plan sequential lessons. Here, teachers take turns in teaching the large group made up of two or three classrooms of children. This makes inservice education more readily available in that teachers may observe each other teach and offer comments for improvement. Smaller groupings of four or five pupils might then work on problems subsequent to large group instruction. Cooperating teachers might then circulate among committees to offer assistance as needed to foster learner interest and meaning in the ongoing activity.

Individual needs must be met, based on the large and small group endeavors. It is good to document needs of pupils which were noticed in the previous grouping arrangements. Each anecdotal statement then is dated per pupil and necessary help given as listed. The mathematics teacher needs to have needed indepth subject matter and pedagogy in mind in order to offer quality guidance. Mastery learning is salient. Pupils individually must attain sequentially. What is not understood needs remedying so that a solid foundation is built for acquiring ensuing mathematical facts, concepts, and generalizations. Too frequently, the teacher has hurried and moved rapidly to cover content in the basal textbook with little attention paid to learner achievement of each step of progress in an ongoing unit of study.

Inservice Growth

Mathematics teachers must possess the needed knowledge to implement high quality strategies of instruction. Growth and achievement is ongoing in teaching. Thus, the public school should have a convenient place for mathematics teachers to study and converse with colleagues on mathematics content and effective means of instruction. In this area for study, there should be recent mathematics journals, yearbooks, and paperbacks published by the National Council Teachers of Mathematics, among others. Encouragement must be given by school administrators for teachers to read and implement ideas which meet standards of quality. The same would be true for housing university level mathematical teacher education texts.

Math teachers may meet together to analyze content and pedagogical methods to improve the curriculum. The dates for meetings and the math literature or topics to be discussed need to be agreed upon. Teachers, also, must elaborate on what has worked well for them pertaining to that used in teaching and learning situations in ongoing lessons and units of study. The doors of effective communication need to be opened among teachers so that good ideas circulate among group members. Trust and consideration for each other is vital. Mathematics teachers and pupils are poignant in the total educational enterprise. Thus, the processes of group work need emphasis. Each can learn much from others and motivate cooperative endeavors. Enthusiasm for learning might well be a motivator to build morale among committee members. New ideas need to be motivated to increase energy levels for teaching mathematics!

Mathematics teachers need to engage in self-reflection in which they:

- rehearse what was achieved previously in teaching pupils in noticing that which may be done differently to optimize progress
- take careful notice of what is needed personally in inservice education to improve teaching performance
- become increasingly proficient in managing grouping procedures as well as learner behaviour.
- must think in terms of continuous improvement of the self as well as of pupils in mathematical content and skills.

Teachers of mathematics need to develop favourable attitudes in curriculum endeavors. A good self-concept must be attained. Thus, self-efficacy is a salient goal in that:

- teachers feel competent in teaching pupils of a variety of achievement and ability levels
- the latest technology can be used very effectively to enhance pupil learning
- they can provide, fully, for individual differences among learners including children of poverty and from diverse cultures
- teaching methods can be used which are beneficial to all English Language Learners (ELL) regardless of language proficiency
- definite provisions can be made to teach diverse categories of handicapped pupils.
- mathematics teachers exhibit pride in their profession when communicating with others.

Mathematics may be integrated with other academic areas, for example, such as the social studies in that learners study Egyptian and Roman systems of numeration; and in science whereby mathematics is the language of the physical sciences as in force, distance, and work performed given in numerical terms. Integration is stressed when there is a need to do so and it assists pupils to understand relevant facts, concepts, and generalizations (Ediger and Rao, 2013).

Evaluation of Achievement

There are selected methods of achievement which need to be used to assess learner progress. Mandated testing occurs once a year and involves the use of standardized tests. Thus, pupils for any grade level have the same directions, time limits, and the same scoring key used in computerized scoring. Validity and reliability data are given in the Manual for each test taken by pupils in the pilot study. The mathematics teacher's pupils score from test results is then compared with those in the Manual to ascertain percentile ranking and/or grade equivalent. Numerical data are then obtained to learn about each pupil's achievement as well as average achievement for a classroom and/or school system. From all testing situations, the teacher needs to use printouts/feedback to notice what needs more emphasis. Errors made by pupils stress the need for remedial work in terms of processes and products. Standardized tests are generally given once a school year; thus, in the mean time, teacher made tests also play a vital role in instruction.

Teacher written tests may also include multiple choice test items whereby the stem with one distractor of four given is correct. However, teacher written tests should include essay items; these include problem solving which broadens pupil's knowledge and skills by having authentic word problems to solve. Here, pupils need to show their work in arriving at the correct answer. The advantages of having pupils show processes include the following:

- the teacher may notice thought processes involved by pupils and thus aid is provided to assist pupils in remediation
- he/she may notice algorithms used by pupils in problem solving
- reading difficulties in solving word problems
- incorrect copying of numerals making for errors
- illegible handwriting making for difficulties to track pupil progress in doing problem solving.

Teacher observation using quality standards of evaluation of pupil work in ongoing lessons, on a daily basis stresses:

- the importance of assisting pupils when difficulties arise in computation and problem-solving. With assistance, adequate time must be given for pupils to analyze, synthesize, and evaluate, to become sett sufficient in remedying difficulties.
- noticing difficulties in individual learner processes to stress remediation in large and small group sessions (Ediger, 2012).

In conclusion

The mathematics curriculum continues to change in terms of subject matter emphasis and methodology in teaching. Quality inservice education is needed to stress the best of objectives for pupil attainment, means for learners to attain these objectives, and appraisal techniques. Education is ongoing and subject to continuous change. Thus, there will always be a need for continuous education.

REFERENCES

Ediger, Marlow (2012), "Towards a High Quality Mathematics Curriculum," *Experiments in Education*, 40(4), 45-46.

Ediger, Marlow, and D. Bhaskara Rao (2013), *Essays on Teaching Mathematics*. New Delhi, India: Discovery Publishing House Pvt. Ltd.

25

Reading in Mathematics Curriculum

Reading word problems may cause difficulties for selected pupils due to their lack of comprehension of print content. Abstract words are more difficult in securing inherent meanings as compared to using manipulative materials. The latter can be seen and touched whereas words are agreed upon symbols which stand for certain facts and ideas. Each pupil must become proficient in reading mathematical subject matter due to its saliency in numeracy and the numerical world. Thus, teachers need to be teachers of reading in mathematics. They need to possess necessary skills to teach word recognition and comprehensions skills in ensuing lessons/units of study in mathematics. Fluency in pupil reading makes for possible increased comprehension of subject matter. Comprehension is hindered when word recognition becomes a problem. Stumbling over words or incorrect identification makes for reading becoming an undesirable task (Ediger and Rao, 2012).

Objectives for Meaning Through Reading

Problems which might arise in word recognition need to be identified prior to or during reading of mathematical content. If identified prior to, then each word chosen by the teacher is selected from the text material and he/she hypothesizes that these will hinder comprehension if left uncorrected. Depending upon the achievement level of the learners involved, the following might be selected: sum, addend, total, minuend, subtrahend, and difference. These need to appear in neat, manuscript style for all to see clearly, be it the class as a whole or within a small group of pupils. The teacher may point to each word and have sequential learners respond in terms of their correct pronunciation. All should participate actively. Their related meanings and use in sentences should also be elaborated upon. The same words may appear on a class word wall for all to see at their leisure. Pupils, individually, might also keep a record of these words, definitions, and within sentences, in a personal mathematics dictionary. When supervising university student teachers in the public schools, the writer noticed how pupils spend brief periods of leisure time studying the words on the word wall, asking questions of each other and of the teacher pertaining to meanings and usage of these words.

There are times when the teacher desires to teach the identification and meaning of unknown words in context. Thus, the teacher asks the pupil in an educated guess what the unknown word is when relating it in context. Pupils might give ridiculous words but realize they do not belong. This may narrow it down to a few words; by viewing the first letter of the unknown plus use of context clues might well make for independent readers. Additional phonics may be utilized as necessary to achieve skill in deciphering the unknown words. Sometimes, the word should be immediately pronounced when the child makes known he/she is stuck on a word. The goal is to assist pupils to work on mathematical problems and not stumble over word recognition.

Meaning must always be present in pursuing objectives in ongoing lessons and units of study. For example when being a fifth grade pupil, the writer learned rote-wise that to divide fractions, one inverts the divisor and multiplies, as was done previously when studying the multiplication of fractions. Thus, questions were not exactly encouraged. Years later, he realized on his own time why one inverts the divisor when dividing fractions. Why is meaning and understanding important? New subject matter generally is built upon and related to previously acquired content. There might be hindrances in understanding the ensuing if previous learnings have been vague or hazy.

To develop problem-solving skills, the mathematics teacher needs to be a leader of inquiry learning. Teachers need to become proficient in the arena of inquiry learning. Thus, the teacher leads pupils through rational thinking procedures involving a solution. He/she must place the self in the place of the pupil when proceeding. These sequential, ordered questions provide a framework for eliciting rational thought in problem solving. Each question is related to the previous pupil response. Learners must have opportunities to think through a possible solution with proper pacing and patience involved. Haste might well make for pupil frustration and a lack of prowess.

Each pupil must be considered as a human being with much worth and the psychology of learning must be utilized to elicit appropriate responses. A firm and relaxed atmosphere should be prevail in teaching and learning situations. If a pupil or pupils does do not come up with sequential responses leading to a mathematical solution to a problem, then very brief explanations in-between should suffice. The spaces in sequence may need to be very small to aid learners in coming up with a correct response, allowing for different algorithms.

Being able to solve problems in mathematics might well be emphasized in collaborative settings. Thus, for example, four pupils may work cooperatively in problem solve situations. Readiness in background information may come from the larger group class as a whole session. One or more problems can be worked upon within the committee, depending upon their complexity. Leadership arises as the need arises to contribute. There are definite criteria which the members need to adhere to so that all are contributing and learning; pupils need to stay on the topic and not digress. Digressing wastes time and is a major cause for some teachers not utilizing committee endeavors. To reiterate, it is poignant for each committee member to contribute actively in problem solving. Depending upon others to do the work makes it so that selected committee members are not learning. Pupils must be polite and considerate of each other; assisting each other to achieve, when needed is definitely advocated. This is a small group endeavor in stressing more optimal attainment. The psychology of constructivism is involved here in that committee members largely sequence their own learnings. If teacher assistance is necessary, then help must be provided so that the committee may move on toward task completion. The solved problem or set of problems may then be given to the teacher for evaluation. Teacher and self-evaluation of committee endeavors are important. Self-evaluation by pupils might include rating the self on a five point scale to notice the reading-discussion connection such as in the following items:

- I participated fully in the discussion. (If there is vagueness in the response to items, these should be made very clear, such as what does it mean to participate fully?)
- I spoke clearly so that others understood what was said. (This, too, will come in degrees. Lack of clarity should be noted and might well provide learnings for ensuing lessons in meaningful oral communication in mathematics.)
- I tried not interrupt others during the discussion.
- I listened carefully to what each pupil was saying (quality listening is a very excellent approach in learning and is highly salient to emphasize in school and in society.)
- I stayed on the topic being discussed.
- I was not distracted from what was happening during the discussion.
- I recommend the following for improving committee work.

  (1) ....

  (2) ....

In Conclusion

Mathematics teachers need to identify when/where pupils need assistance in word recognition in the numeracy arena.

Help must be provided as necessary in developing fluency and analytical readers. Pupils need to achieve objectives of instruction through high quality learning experiences. Evaluation procedures must be valid and reliable to provide feedback for ensuing lessons and units of study (Ediger, 2007).

REFERENCES

Ediger, Marlow (2007), Teacher Observation to Assess Achievement," *Journal of Instructional Psychology*, 34(3), 137- 139.

Ediger, Marlow, and D. Bhaskara Rao (2012), *Essays on Teaching Mathematics*. New Delhi, India: Discovery Publishing House Pvt. Ltd.

26

Teaching Science, Key Elements of Instruction

To optimize achievement, the science teacher needs to follow selected suggestions in teaching and learning situations. These suggestions follow the psychology of education in assisting pupil progression through the grades as well as guide learners to do well in STEM.

Key Items in the Science Curriculum

In my 30 years of supervising university student teachers in the public schools, there are certain features of teaching which invite learner participation.

First, experiments and demonstrations should be at the heart of science instruction. They need to be well-planned and arranged so that all pupils might observe carefully what transpires when testing hypotheses. Lack of visibility, jumping to hasty conclusions, and taking the teacher's word as to outcomes violates selected tenets of objectivity so necessary in science.The hypotheses, ideally, should come from learners.

Second, large group and smaller committees need formation to discuss indepth as to what happened in the science experiments and demonstrations. The verification principle is poignant in science and within collaborative settings, pupils may challenge each other's statements in terms of being fact or opinion, fantasy or reality. Pupils, in these situations, learn from each other and from the science teacher who serves as salient guide. Critical thinking is important as well as creative thought. The latter stresses originality, which is very important in coming up with novel, unique ideas from which society benefits in time/place with inventions and methods. Appropriate standards need development and used to appraise the ongoing collaboration. Presenting subject matter with clarity and listening carefully to each other is vital in good oral communication endeavors.

Third, reading content with meaning and understanding is highly relevant. The science teacher needs to be a teacher of reading so that important facts, concepts, and generalizations may be acquired by pupils. Word recognition is a problem which selected pupils experience. Thus, several procedures need to be in the offing to assist pupils in recognizing unknown words. A most important strategy is to utilize context clues. Here, the learner is to fill in a word which makes sense in place of the unknown. If a pupil gives a ridiculous word, he/she must realize this does not make for meaning. If this is not adequate, the pupil needs to sound out the initial consonant of the unknown. Context clues and the initial consonant sound should do it, if not additional phonic sounds need to be looked at. The recommended approach here should be to spend as little time as possible on word recognition techniques so that comprehension of subject matter is possible. Sometimes, it might be a good procedure to immediately pronounce the unknown to the involved pupil which then aids in encouraging interest and sequence in reading content. The use of picture clues (the illustration on the printed page may provide needed hints), as well as configuration clues (shape and form of the unknown). The major purpose of reading is to attach meaning to subject matter read (Essays in Teaching Reading, 2012).

Fourth, to reiterate, reading critically and creatively are two leading goals of comprehension in reading science subject matter, but there are other objectives such as

- developing a main idea with supporting details
- summarizing and drawing conclusions of what was read
- giving an oral/written report on a selected, salient topic in an ongoing science unit of study

- writing up what transpired in a committee meeting. This shows the reading/writing connection.
- doing a voluntary book report on a related science topic.

Fifth, Pupils need to keep a science notebook of important happenings within sequential lessons and units of study. These need to possess dated entries of science experiments, records of readings in science, related library books read, reports written, science art work, digital images of projects completed, teacher written test results, and data from standardized test results, among others. An expanded form of this would be the portfolio. These artifacts provide information for parent/ teacher conferences. Parents might then observe first hand the quality of work completed by the pupil. From the discussion, parents, the teacher, and the child might well come up with objectives to be achieved. Progress may be noticed during the time interval involving later conferences. Positive parental involvement is to be encouraged!

Sixth, qualitative habits and manners need careful consideration since they do effect classroom environment and personal conduct. Attitudes toward the self such as the self-concept is of utmost importance. A good self-concept aids achievement in all academic areas, science included. Science as a curriculum area needs to be prized very highly. Living in a world of science, it is so necessary to work toward improvement in all facets of life and living. Medical science has made tremendous headways with a longer healthier life span possible, but it still has a long ways to find cures or that which minimizes cancer, heart attacks, strokes, allergies, and the common cold, among others. Then too, with the world of work being made easier and less labor intensive including inventions of self-propelled combines to harvest grain in very large acreages, eighteen wheelers to haul heavy loads of cargo over long distances, grain augurs to load farm crops onto trucks without the use of hand shovels to shovel grain, among many other labour saving devices. Labour intensive harvesting farm crops include strawberries for which no invention has been found as yet to minimize strenuous manual labour.

Seventh, a high quality assessment programme must be emphasized to ascertain learner achievement. This is true of teacher written science tests, standardized mandated tests, among the more formal procedures. Thus, tests must be valid in that they measure what it states will be measured. Thus a science test desiring to ascertain pupil progress in setting up and doing experiments must measure knowledge, skills, and attitudes therein. There have been science tests whose purpose was to measure pupil progress in problem-solving, but instead stressed factual knowledge only. Thus, an invalid test was used. Tests must also be reliable in that if learners take a test in science, they basically receive the same/similar percentile the second time the test its taken. Alternate forms and split half reliability data given in the Manual of the standardized test are also acceptable. Less formal means of appraisal of pupil achievement include:

- anecdotal statements, dated and written by the teacher, to show actual attainment of each pupil
- science art projects include murals, bulletin board displays, drawings, diagrams, and posters
- creative written products as in writing diverse forms of poetry using science content
- graphs, tables, and charts to indicate science data with teacher observation and supervision to notice gains (Ediger, 2010).

REFERENCES

Ediger, Marlow (2010), "Children's Literature in the Science Curriculum," *Journal of Instructional Psychology*, 37(2), 117-119.

Ediger, Marlow, and D. Bhaskara Rao (2012), *Essays on Teaching Reading*. New Delhi, India: Discovery Publishing House Pvt. Ltd.

27

The Changing Science Curriculum

Science, as a curriculum area, has gone through many changes recently with the oncoming of the Common Core State Standards (CCSS), Science, Technology, Engineering, and Mathematics (STEM), as well as the Next Generation Science Standards (NGSS).

Science is a part of everyday life which individuals experience. Even the drying up of a puddle of water after a rainfall has a definite scientific explanation. We certainly live in a world of science. Science has brought on tremendous changes in society with improved medical findings and services thus promoting a longer and healthier life span for many; labor saving devices with automation and hydraulic/electrical devices to perform work; automatic teller machines for instant access cash, as well as online banking services; farming with air conditioned cabs on tractors and combines, and hydraulic lifts for plowing and seeding. Heavy manual labor has been eliminaded or greatly minimized.

A modern science curriculum must be in the offing for each pupil in the school setting. This is vital to prepare learners for college as well as the work place.

Developing the Science Curriculum

Inquiry learning is at the heart of ongoing science lessons and units of study. This is opposite of rote learning. With inquiry learning, pupils achieve facts, concepts, and generalizations indepth. Questions raised by pupils need to be encouraged which stimulate achievement and aid in the inquiry process. The identified questions might well lead into problem solve experiences. Problems here need to possess clarity so that an ensuing hypothesis might be developed which is capable of being tested. A variety of experiences provide the testing experience in that the hypothesis results in being accepted, rejected, or need of modification. This takes time to develop the hypothesis, test it, and assess the results. The process cannot be hurried since much data gathering is involved in each of these flexible steps (Ediger, 2013).

It becomes necessary to reflect upon the processes and notice which actions come next in sequence as well as what needs to be improved upon from previous experiences. Reflective thinking is a highly worthwhile goal for all in the societal realm. It assists one to review/rehearse previous actions in terms of making possible revisions. Also, knowledge and skills are put to use in these situations.

Reflection, too, aids in arriving at what is truly salient to learn. Structural ideas are poignant in any academic discipline, science included. Structure provides a foundation which provides support for ensuing objectives being achieved. New ideas acquired then become related to the structure. Thus, supporting ideas or a broadening of structural content is in the offing. Supporting ideas provide a firmer structure since they strengthen the structure.

Experimentation needs to be central in ongoing science lessons and units of study. Pupils with teacher guidance need to be involved in setting up and doing the experiments. One variable needs to be tested at a given time which then eliminates others. The experiment needs to be clearly visible to all who are participating. Learners must hypothesize as to outcomes but not jump to hasty conclusions. Careful and meticulous observation is needed. Hindrances to pupil achievement need to be eliminated so that pupils might focus upon the objectives. Testing the hypothesis and reaching accurate conclusions are necessary to secure valid and reliable results. The experiment or a related one may be done to check conclusions realized. Subject matter from other reputable, developmental sources may also enter in to the discussion. This might well include basal textbook sources.

When reading science subject matter, meaning is salient; otherwise it delimits comprehension. Indepth comprehension is the major objective of reading. Pupils need to be able to verify their answers to questions/problems when reading content. The science teacher must be a teacher of reading to assist pupils in fluent reading. This involves word recognition which might cause problems to selected students. Thus, the teacher needs to guide pupils in utilizing:

- structural analysis in word identification in that a word given by the learner for the unknown makes sense contextually in relationship to surrounding words.
- phonics whereby a pupil sounds out letters in the unknown word to come up with the correct word.
- picture clues, especially for the young child in which illustrations appear on almost every page of science content. The illustration may prove the correct word for the unknown by reading the related pictures.
- graphs and charts on the page being read which contain the unknown word. They can provide much information on individual words to be deciphered as well as in general knowledge related directly to indepth learning of subject matter.

For young children, textbook content may be read collectively with the guidance of the science teacher. Thus by following along in the textbook, the pupil notices each word as the small group reads aloud. Struggling readers on higher grade levels, too, have benefited from using this procedure. It avoids embarrassment for those who misidentify enough words to hinder comprehension. The goal is to aid pupils to become fluent readers, attain relevant facts, concepts, and generalizations, as well as develop favorable attitudes toward science. When working in small groups, pupils may assist each other in word identification problems. They might also read aloud the contents to listeners in a groups of three to five or work in dyads with two learners involved.

When working in small groups or the class as a whole, the following guidelines re poignant to follow:

- respect the thinking of contributions made.
- clarify ideas not understood.
- have all participate, if possible.
- stay on the topic being pursued; do not stray to the irrelevant.
- no one should dominate the discussion (Ediger and Rao, 2012).

Technology in Science

Technology has much to offer in improving teaching and learning situations. Its use should optimize science achievement. Thus, technology in its diverse forms needs to assist pupils to:

- attain vital objectives of instruction
- provide for individual differences
- provide guidance in evaluation of achievement with validity and reliability in mind.

REFERENCES

Ediger, Marlow (2013), "Science-An Indepth Approach", *Connecticut Journal of Science Education*, 50 (2), 5-7.

Ediger, Marlow, and D. Bhaskara Rao (2012), *Essays on Teaching Science*. New Delhi, India: Discovery Publishing House Pvt. Ltd.

28

New Science Curriculum

Each academic discipline must be updated due to changes in school and in society; science is no exception. Diverse groups, organizations, and councils are busy in looking at necessary modifications and changes. New programmes of science instruction then emerge. Pupils need to work as scientists do at the work place and this might well prepare persons to work in the different fields of science and technology. Objectivity is a key concept when engaged in the world and workings of science.

Experimentation in Science

Experiments and experimentation must be the core of the science curriculum. Pupils need to be heavy involved in the development of experiments. These must be clear for all to see when looking at conclusions and evidence. Arguing from evidence becomes a major objective here. Focusing upon the experiment becomes paramount. Too frequently, pupils jump to hasty conclusions and fail to view each experiment objectively. To develop rational conclusions, the learner must argue from observed evidence. Pupils may work in small groups to consider each other's observations of the experiment. The hypotheses, written on the board, should come from individual pupils. The teacher, if needed, clarifies a response given by a learner. Clarification might also come from learners as they sharpen their individual hypotheses. Generating of ideas, from evidence, is poignant here, and each will be tested through verification.

Looking what experts say is also an approach used in testing hypotheses. The experts may be authors of the basal texts utilized in class. Reading to secure information on each hypothesis is a necessary skill to develop within pupils. Fluency in reading subject matter must be a salient objective for pupils to attain. The science instructor as well as the language arts teacher may harmonize teaching procedures in developing rich science vocabularies within pupils. The science teacher may instruct in the following ways, among others:

- use of context clues to identify unknown words with the individual intended meanings
- use of salient phonics learnings to identify the unknown word
- have word walls in the classroom for pupils to reflect upon and utilize new words in science
- assist pupil to develop a vocabulary section of science words in their individual notebooks
- utilize new words in science reports
- do voluntary summarizing of individual readings in science (for extra credit)
- use of new words by the teacher in teaching and learning situations (Ediger and Rao, 2012).

Vocabulary development is of utmost importance in ongoing lessons and units of study. Relevant use must be made of these terms. The teacher and pupils must plan to incorporate scientific vocabulary in contextual situations into speaking, listening, reading, and writing experiences. Informational library books should have introductions provided to children which whet appetites for reading. These books may be read orally to children on younger age levels. They might also provide relevant knowledge for older aged pupils who need assistance in word recognition and comprehension. Following along in the book as the script is being read aloud meets needs of selected pupils.

Experience charts are good to develop for vocabulary achievement for young children, as well as those who do not read well. For example, primary grade children might view an experiment on their understanding level. Based on objective observations made, the pupils may present content based upon these observations. The science teacher may record what is being said orally. Pupils then see talk written down. These pupils may then read their own ideas pertaining to a science experiment. The science teacher appraises understandings accrued by learners. This gives pupils a chance to read their very own ideas, presented aloud, as well as read together with the teacher in following the abstract print. In this way, pupils might well experience success in reading which should assist in attaching meaning to more complex understandings. Sequential progress in reading science content is relevant and builds confidence in ongoing lessons and units of study. A good self concept is salient for young children as they pursue structural and supporting concepts. Then too, struggling readers on higher grade levels, also, may comprehend subject matter with the experience chart philosophy.

Critical thinking is important in that pupils at an early age need to separate accurate from inaccurate ideas. Time spent here is time well spent. In science and in everyday life situations, pupils need to seek, explore, and implement accuracy in thought. In addition to accuracy, pupils need to separate what is relevant from the irrelevant. This is especially true in problem-solving. When viewing an experiment, pupils need guidance to argue the important from the non-important in seeking answers. Passively accepting opinions as facts does not harmonize with the scientific method of learning. Rather, opinions definitely must be sorted out as being non-scientific. Experiments and their conclusions must be verified with a philosophy of objectivity.

Creative thinking seeks the novel, new, and original in thought and must be respected. Originality in ideas may become hypotheses to be tested with the possibility that new discoveries in science might well come about.

Collaborative settings provide opportunities for small groups to discuss science experiment results. Reading content from a carefully chosen science textbook might also be emphasized in a committee setting. Close reading is necessary to extract meaning from the passages. Answers to problem areas and questions might well be resolved through verification from the textbook source. Other information sources may be brought in as needed to check hypotheses and answers to questions. Working as scientists, learners need to read accurately and precisely to secure data needed. Structural and supporting ideas need focus with careful reading and critical thinking to come up with what is accurate. Pupils must come up with that which represents regularity with careful reasoning.

Inservice education is necessary for teachers to adopt and accept new, innovative procedures of science instruction. Beliefs may need modification so that science teachers function effectively in innovative procedures. The objectives of instruction need to be understood meaningfully so they can be implemented to secure optimal learner progress. These need to be ordered and paced effectively to secure pupil attention. Assistance must be provided if teachers do not attach meaning to pedagogy at any stage of implementation. The following, among others, may be utilized in inservice education:

- workshops which focus clearly upon lessons and units to be taught
- faculty meetings devoted to science instruction. These clarify specific problems identified by science teachers
- independent studies which emphasize innovations in science teaching
- enrolment in science education classes at an accredited university
- taking an online course in science pedagogy
- demonstration teaching in a specific science lesson.

Listening as a way of learning is often neglected in the school setting. High quality listening is a poignant goal to attain in the science curriculum, being valuable across the different academic areas. How might the teacher developing good listening habits when pupils are turned off in an ongoing lesson? The teacher's voice can do much to secure learner attention. Pitching selected words within a sentence, appropriately, at different levels might well incorporate learner attention. A monotone or unenthused teaching voice certainly will not help the learning process. Linguists have analyzed the saliency of voice inflection and its affect in teaching. A word may be spoken softly or in ascending loudness. Then too, pausing briefly at appropriate sequential places stresses the importance of chosen words to indicate what is poignant. There are punctuation marks which indicate the kinds of expressed sentences in printed script such as interrogative, imperative, exclamatory, and declarative. In oral communication, the communicator must utilize voice inflection in expressing meaning to the listener. Thus, the communicator has an obligation to speak clearly in collaborative settings so that listeners had ample opportunities to comprehend facts, concepts, and generalizations.

Listeners too have an equal obligation to understand messages. Pupils need to develop a mind set which encourages good listening. The science teacher might well assist in establishing goals for listening and then periodically evaluate with learners if the objectives are being attained. Self-appraisal by each pupil is also recommenced. Individuals lose out in life in securing information due to faulty listening habits. Listening with a purpose in mind is important! The following purposes need adequate emphasis:

- pupil's raising questions about a science experiment and these questions become purposes for listening during a large or small group discussion.
- verification of information obtained provides for interaction among pupils in the classroom setting
- hypothesizing stresses high quality listening habits.

The science teacher may structure an activity which requires good listening by stating the following, flexible questions:

- which understandings should pupils attain, i.e. what is the major finding to look for in an ongoing experiment?
- what should be omitted an experiment so that only one variable is being tested?
- how can an hypothesis be stated so that it truly tests for an objective outcome?
- what might be done to verify or refute an hypothesis?
- how should the findings of an experiment be utilized?

In each discussion, the quality of evaluation must be assessed so that knowledge and skills increase and these provide background experiences for ensuing leanings in science lessons and units of study. Listening is a very important part of achievement, and teachers and pupils must appraise the quality of these endeavors (Ediger, 2010).

REFERENCES

Ediger, Marlow (2010), The Pupil, Writing, and the Science Curriculum, *Experiments in Education*, 38 (4), 19-22.

Ediger, Marlow, and D. Bhaskara Rao (2012), *Essays on Teaching Science*. New Delhi, India: Discovery Publishing House.

29

Science and Reading within Indepth Problem-solving

Objectives in ongoing science lessons and units of study need to incorporate reading skills, since the latter is salient in securing needed scientific information. Otherwise the focal point is upon essential scientific knowledge, skills, and attitudes for pupil attainment. Teachers need to choose carefully which vital ends learners are to achieve. Relevant facts, concepts, and generalizations might well provide structure within each unit of study. Scientific thinking is poignant in school and in society and pervades all curriculum areas. Objectivity is a key or central belief in the science domain.

Reading in Science

To achieve well in ongoing science lessons and units of study, the pupils must improve reading comprehension to assist in confirming conclusions from science experiments, teacher demonstrations in experimentation, as well as help to secure information for problems and questions identified by learners. Adequate background information needs to be in the offing for the ensuing activity. Thus, pupils need to understand selected facts and main ideas inherent in the reading experience. By using concrete objects, video tapes, and illustrations, pupils have a better chance of understanding the related subject matter. They may identify new words in print which might provide difficulties in word recognition. These may be printed in neat, manuscript style on the chalk/

whiteboard and pronounced aloud; this will maximize fluency in reading and aid comprehension. For individuals, the science teacher may help a learner identify an unknown word by asking for a word which makes sense in relationship to the other words in the sentence or paragraph. If this is not adequate, ask the pupil what sound stands for the first letter in the unknown. The first letter will generally be a consonant and these are very consistent between symbol and sound. This procedure eliminates many unknown words in reading for meaning. Additional phonic learnings may be stressed as the need arises (Ediger and Rao, 2012). The ultimate goal is comprehension and to comprehend ideas for problem solving. Additional procedures to utilize in identifying unknown words are the following:

- for young children in particular, a picture in the textbook may give away what the unknown word is in recognition.
- have dyads at work in the classroom whereby two pupils read together from the text and decipher the unknown words. In providing practice in identifying sight words, flash cards might also be used in which two pupils change off with one holding the sequential cards while the other pronounces that word correctly. These leanings should transfer to improved reading in problem-solving.
- a committee of learners may assist each other in collaborative reading of content.
- a good reader may pronounce correctly unknown words to a pupil; here, the learner may move on quickly to sequential reading of ideas for problem solving.
- use an overhead projector in helping pupils in reading text materials whereby all can clearly see the subject matter on the screen in collaborative oral reading lead by the science teacher.

Once pupils identify words correctly, then fluency and comprehension of text materials will improve. At the same time, pupils read subject matter, questions and problems arise.

The text might be utilized, as one source, to secure information. Verification of answers/solutions is necessary. Doing science experiments is an approach to check conclusions from reading sequential sources, as well as *vice versa*. The experiment must be set up so that all can see clearly what is transpiring. Hypotheses need developing as temporary solutions to the problem. Jumping to hasty conclusions needs to be substituted for gathering objective evidence. Thus, the science experiment in and of itself provides the evidence, not personal biases nor prejudices. Experiments should include the following standards:

- emphasize a major objective, not trivia
- be on the developmental levels of involved learners
- enhance pupil motivation and effort. Too frequently, learners are turned off on dull and repetitive experimentations
- build on knowledge and skills presently possessed
- have plans for sequential learning activities for pupils
- assist learners in utilizing new knowledge and skills in ensuing science units and in life in society
- at all times, help pupils to think scientifically within the framework of teaching and learning. Identification of problems, developing hypotheses, evaluating an hypothesis, and achieve an objective conclusion (Ediger, 2010).

Language Arts in the Science Curriculum

Pupils need to become good listeners in collaborative settings. High quality listening assists in building upon previously acquired information and skills. It also helps pupils to extend to achieve critical and creative thinking skills. There needs to be a question/problem for meticulous listening on the part of the pupil. Especially if it comes from the learner, do pupils perceive purpose or reasons for listening. Intrinsically, this provides motivation for listening to occur. Motivation, or a higher energy level for listening, is necessary to connect and stay connected. There are a plethora of distractions in any classroom, and problem solving must receive major emphasis here. Criteria for good listening may be developed by pupils with teacher guidance and posted on the wall where all may view its contents. Periodically, pupils with teacher assistance need to appraise how well these standards are being met. Criteria may be omitted/modified or added. The goal here is to develop good listening habits.

Clear oral communication aids in achieving quality in listening. Thus, proper stress, pitch, and enunciation need to be in the offing. Asking salient questions and identifying important problems might well be modeled by the teacher. Increased knowledge/skills in science assists in doing well in oral communication.

Then too, written products in science are highly significant in that scientists, as a model, communicate effectively with others. The following are written products, in which technology including the word processor are very functional:

- keeping record of science experiments
- doing and keeping a file of book reports and essay test results
- developing log and diary entries

There are a plethora of uses for computers, i-Pads, i-Phones, in the science curriculum. Technology and its maintenance/upkeep is expensive; wise decisions must be made here in its purchase and utilization, by implementing the following criteria:

- it must assist pupils in attaining vital goals in science lessons and units of study.

- it needs to provide for individual differences among learners
- it should provide ample opportunities for problem-solving, critical and creative thinking
- it emphasizes the achievement of high quality attitudes.

REFERENCES

Ediger, Marlow (2010), "Children's Literature in the Science Curriculum," *Journal of Instructional Psychology*, 37(2), 117-119.

Ediger, Marlow, and D. Bhaskara Rao (2012), *Essays on Teaching Science*. New Delhi, India: Discovery Publishing House Pvt. Ltd.

30

Reading, Science and the Pupil

Reading along with science experiments are vital approaches in learning in ensuing lessons and units of study. Reading is more abstract and symbols stand for words and meanings. Scientific literacy is very important in gathering and organizing information pertaining to answering questions as well as finding solutions to problems. Fluency in reading is a must in order for the pupil to obtain needed facts, concepts, and generalizations. Words can be too complex for reading; strategies then need to be ascertained to identify words and their meanings. Thus, the science teacher must have adequate knowledge and skills to assist learners to comprehend subject matter.

Teaching Science and Reading

Text materials in science need to be read in a meaningful manner in order for comprehension to occur. How might the science teacher assist pupils with word recognition problems? If a pupil is "stuck" on a word, he/she may be helped in using context clues. For example, pupils might provide outlandish words for the unknown; these do not make sense and the pupil can see that by listening to his/her efforts. Additional help in word recognition may be provided by the teacher by having the pupil look at the first consonant letter and sounding it out when utilizing context clues. Sequential learnings in phonics can make for independence in word recognition and thus stress independence in reading fluently, the goal being to become proficient readers and not be hindered with unknown words. Additional word recognition techniques include the following:

- use of picture clues, especially for young children when illustrations are generally numerous. For instance, a pupil does not recognize the abstract word, but referring to the illustration on that page provides the necessary clue.
- use of configuration clues, might help in that the shape of the word provides needed help (Ediger and Rao, 2012).

When questions and problems arise in reading textual materials, answers and solutions might be located therein, through "close reading". This requires reading indepth and rereading to verify subject matter. Verification might also come in through other experiences including experimentation in science. Reflective thinking assists in having pupils rethink what has been learned. Providing clarity of what has been read, experimentation is at the heart of science instruction; these should be clearly visible to all so that conclusions may be realized through pupil observation. Redoing an experiment helps to clarify secured information. To increase understanding of facts, concepts, and generalizations read in depth, the teacher might show and discuss, with learners, a related video-tape. The video-tape, briefly introduced to guide learners to perceive the relationship to the ongoing lesson/ unit of study helps to visualize selected concepts such as gully and sheet erosion, grassed waterways to prevent erosion, terracing of farm land, as well as planting of trees. Reading of pictures from the video-tape as well as listening to the audio or hearing part enhances achievement, providing that stimulation of interest is prevalent. There are pupils who pay little attention to illustrations in text materials along with other visuals, and thus lose out on opportunities to learn. Graphs, charts, and tables, too, must be read carefully to provide needed information related to the script or abstract word (Ediger, 2013).

What has been read must be used in diverse ways such as in a discussion. These might be the class as a whole or a small group endeavor. In either situation, pupils need to:

- stay on the topic, generally using complete sentences in communicating ideas orally. It is vital that quality is inherent in using oral language to state ideas clearly so that listeners understand and attach meaning to comments made.
- assist all to contribute. Discussions might falter if a few monopolize the discussion; others may then tune out.
- clarify vague content to assist in generating ideas and subject matter.
- guide learners to move forward during the discussion and not develop feelings of not knowing how to proceed.
- avoid behaviours which hinder progress. These behaviours include rudeness, intimidation, put downs, and abrasive remarks.

When in a small group of four to five pupils, leadership can emerge within the group; a recorder should be appointed to present findings to other committees. It is poignant to be a contributing committee member so that learners find collaborative endeavors to be a high quality approach and procedure in learning. Effective oral communication behaviours need cultivation and implementation. The oral communication-reading connection needs to be emphasized. Then too, clarity in written expression, also, needs emphasis. Pupils should do much writing in science as in:

- writing summaries of committee endeavors.
- recording conclusions from science experiments. These need to be thorough and accurate.
- maintaining a diary of classroom activities covering a period of time.
- doing book reports on famous scientists.

- evaluating classroom science experiences in terms of standards.

The language arts areas of reading, writing, and speaking harmonize well with the science curriculum. Listening carefully needs to be integrated and tends to be a forgotten art. The following listening standards are good to stress in ongoing lessons in science:

- have a purpose for listening, such as "We need to understand the three states of matter as in liquids, solids, and gases. I will ask from you to explain each after our discussion."
- emphasize a hands on approach in learning whereby pupils are actively involved in doing science experiments.
- stress the importance of securing directions the first time they are given. For example, have a pupil repeat the directions orally for selected pupils who failed to obtain them the first time. Clarity in giving directions is paramount.
- paraphrase content not presented accurately or with clarity.
- speak so all can hear, but not too loudly which hinders listening comprehension.
- evaluate listening comprehension with questions raised of pupils over subject matter covered.

Quality listening is salient in school and in society. Much repeating and reviewing is necessary due to poor listening habits. As adults, many are embarrassed when they find it necessary to have a question or comments repeated. The reading-listening comprehension connection is important. What is read in science is discussed and needs indepth understanding.

Electronic Books

Electronic books, E Books, have made considerable classroom headways in their being used. They have a plethora of advantages over the regular traditional texts. With adequate background experiences, the pupil can move forward at his/her own rate of speed. The content can be set to read aloud while the pupil follows the script. Thus, there is no hesitating over unknown words to identify; fluency in reading is then in evidence. In the mind of the learner, the subject matter might well be sequential. Unknown words are learned as the print is being followed. Words which lack meaning may be viewed almost immediately on the monitor in terms of a contextual definition. Sidebar questions may guide pupil comprehension as the reading activity progresses. Illustrations, also, assist pupil understanding of subject matter read.

The E-book reader is a blessing to many pupils. For the gifted/talented pupil, traditional text materials might still be highly motivating since these pupils are more independent in their reading capabilities.

REFERENCES

Ediger, Marlow (2013). "Philosophies of Reading Instruction," *Reading Improvement*, 50(3), 132-134.

Ediger, Marlow, and D. Bhaskara Rao (2012), *Essays on Teaching Science*. New Delhi, India: Discovery Publishing House Pvt. Ltd.

31

Changing Social Studies Curriculum

The social studies is undergoing considerable change since the Common Core State Standards (CCSS) are being implemented in the school setting. Prior to the ensuing CCSS, the No Child Left Behind (NCLB) was the law of the land for public schools since 2002 with its complete omission of history and the social studies in its testing component. Thus, the teaching of history/social studies was minimized since teachers tended to focus upon what was being tested and that was being taught. Thus, reading/language arts and mathematics were the only curriculum areas being tested with science also entering the testing scene in 2008, under NCLB.

History and the social studies will have some catching up to do with emphasis upon high quality instruction. Leaders in social studies education have done much work in developing a framework to fit in with the CCSS (Ediger and Rao, 2012).

The C3 Framework of College, Career, and Civics

The C3 Framework (college, career, and civics) provides guidelines for possible inclusion into CCSS. General objectives are listed for pupils to achieve which indicate the direction of learning, and these include the following pertaining to Inquiry Literacies:

1. Questioning
2. Selecting sources

3. Gathering information from sources
4. Evaluating sources
5. Making claims
6. Using evidence
7. Constructing arguments and explanations
8. Adapting arguments and explanations
9. Presenting arguments and explanations
10. Critiquing arguments and explanations
11. Analyzing social problems
12. Assessing options for action
13. Taking informed action (Lee and Swan, 2013).

By looking at the above listed items, it is quite obvious that rote learning and memorization are not emphasized, but rather that pupils learn to think in their various dimensions. Problem-solving is stressed with its contributing goals of identification of problems, securing and evaluating necessary information for possible solutions, and testing the possible solutions (hypotheses) in lifelike and abstract situations. In 2010, the National Council for the Social Studies (NCSS), identified ten themes which are useful in making subject matter decisions, and these are the following:

1. Culture: the study of culture and cultural diversity
2. Time, Continuity, and Change: the study of the past and its legacy
3. People, Places, and Environment: a study of people, places, and environments
4. Individual Development and Identity
5. Individuals, Groups, and Institutions. A study of interactions among individuals, groups, and institutions
6. Power, authority, and Governance. The study of how people create, interact with, and change structures of power, authority, and governance

7. Production, distribution, and consumption. The study of how people organize for Production, Distribution, and Consumption of goods and services
8. Science, Technology, and Society
9. Global Connections. A study of interdependence of people and nations
10. Civic Ideals and Practices. The study of ideals, principles, and practices of citizenship in a democratic republic.

The above-enumerated items provide a broad framework for making rational decisions on subject matter inclusion in teaching and learning situations. Each may be clarified resulting in clearly stated objectives of instruction. Rational balance among these itemized statements might well provide necessary objectives of instruction which assist in providing readiness for making career and college entry decisions. They might well fit into the C3 Framework in lesson and unit development. Item # 10 above, in particular, emphasizes guidelines and their implementation for participants in society. The others, also, contribute to good citizenship such as item #6 above which deal with the powers of government in regulations pertaining to a democratic society.

The CCSS are based upon research in terms of what students need in order to be successful and prepared for the work place as well as course work at colleges and universities. This provides a sound basis for making educational decisions. Quality research might well provide the needed criteria to be used in teaching and learning situations in assisting in the development of successful achievers. This information may then be harmonized with what colleges/universities and the workplace require. A well designed survey may provide needed results for higher education as well as the work place when ascertaining which learnings are necessary for students. Thus, comparisons may be made with results from other states in the nation. Frameworks from the National Assessment of Educational Progress (NAEP) assisted in providing guidelines for reading and writing, both of which are poignant in teaching the social studies.

Clarity was involved in writing the CCSS aligned with college and career readiness. Higher order thinking skills are stresses through acquisition of salient subject matter. These might be utilized in school and in society.

REFERENCES

Ediger, Marlow, and D. Bhaskara Rao (2012), *Essays on Teaching the Social Studies*. New Delhi, India: Discovery Publishing House Pvt. Ltd.

Lee, John, and Kathy Swan, "The C3 Framework, Is the common core good for Social Studies? Yes, but..." *Social Education*, 77(6), 329.

32
New Social Studies Curriculum

As society changes, so must social studies be updated. The utilization of relevant technology has had major input into the curriculum. Pupils of all socio-economic levels must have ample opportunities to use technological advances in ongoing lessons and units of study. Too frequently, low income learners do not possess the opportunities of working with computers in the home setting and the white board, among others, unless provided by the public school. Wherever one goes in the business world, computers are being used, and each pupil needs to keep up with present trends in the societal arena.

There is a danger in the school setting, that technology for its own sake will be emphasized. Rather, it should be utilized to assist pupils to achieve objectives of instruction in a more meaningful manner. Thus, what is learned needs to make sense and be useful. Along with other technological progress, which additional trends make for a new social studies curriculum?

Updating the Social Studies

From teacher observation, discussions, and test results, the social studies teacher is able to tell what pupils do not understand and what needs reteaching or modification. Major concepts and generalizations from each lesson and unit are salient for learner understanding and these present structural ideas for subject matter being emphasized. Subordinate content support the structure, in this approach, pupils also may be guided to relate ensuing ideas to those previously acquired.

There needs to be a school environment which encourages and fosters learning and this element is learner interest. Thus, interesting learning activities assist pupils in becoming absorbed in these experiences. If learners are bored and disinterest is apparent, the chances are little progress, if any, will be shown. Wholehearted involvement through activities vitalizes the social studies and guides pupils in attaining objectives of instruction. Teacher observation is necessary to ascertain the degree of learner involvement in the classroom. If learner interests are starting to wane, then modification or new experiences need to be in the offing. It is indeed challenging for the teacher to meet individual, changing needs of pupils.

The psychology of learning must be stressed in ongoing lessons and units of study. By emphasizing these criteria, teachers help pupil to grow, learn, and achieve. Thus, pupils need to experience:

- purpose in learning whereby he/she perceives relevant subject matter. Subject matter then is usable in diverse contexts. It is useful in ensuing lessons and units of study, and is useful in other curriculum areas, as well as in the societal realm. When relevancy is then perceived, motivation increases and an increased energy level for learning accrues.
- meaning is attached to concepts and generalizations attained. These are not memorized but are understood through questions raised by the teacher as well as other pupils. In daily assessments, formative evaluation, as well as in end of unit tests, pupils and the teacher can verify that learning has been accomplished. There are a plethora of methods whereby pupils might well reveal what has been learned, in addition to testing, and that method is through discussions. Lively discussions involving large groups as well as in small committees provide opportunities

for all pupils to share ideas gleaned from a lesson or unit of study.

- motivation to learn stresses a desire to learn more on a given topic. Effort is then put forth to achieve more optimally. Scaffolding enters into the equation. The teacher then emphasizes learning activities which inspire and stimulate. Encouraging the learner to try and put forth energy to accomplish aids the feeling dimension of the learner. Quality attitudes then might well be on the horizon. Contrast this situation with a pupil who wastes time in getting to work in a given experience. Time is valuable and must be utilized wisely in assisting pupils to attain objectives of instruction (Ediger and Rao, 2012).

Relating subject matter to what is being taught helps learners to make connections within the different academic disciplines. In the social studies, the diverse disciplines may include the following:

- *history.* Important concepts and generalizations comprising a social studies unit of study should come from history. Each nation or country being studied has salient historical events which distinguishes itself from others. These important events, not trivia, must be inherent ingoing lessons and units of study.
- *geography.* Each social studies unit occurs within a region, nation, state, or specific place whereby differences in elevation reveal mountains, hills, plains, plateaus, types of soil, bodies of water, among other differences. Climatic differences and agricultural products produced also vary.
- *economics.* Among other things, this pertains to gross national product of a region/area being studied, goods and services produced, exports and imports, as well as inherent economic enterprises such as concepts of production and distribution.
- *sociology* with emphasis of how cultures are alike as well as different. These may be studied in terms of

foods produced, types of clothing worn, patterns of housing, languages spoken, art, music, as well as architecture.

- *political science.* Rules and regulations as well as laws stressed in government. Local, stale, and federal governments become focal points of study. Being a good citizen with the study of civics is also included.

Social studies teachers need to choose carefully which of the above-named academic disciplines, in degrees, best serve lesson and unit development. Pupils need to become good citizens and have an excellent knowledge of subject matter content to be well informed persons.

Reading, primary and secondary sources, provides an important learning activity to have learners grasp salient ideas in the social studies. Social studies teachers must be good reading instructors so that pupils become more proficient in attaining important knowledge and skills. Word recognition causes difficulties in comprehension and thus, the following needs emphasis:

- *context clues.* If a word causes difficulties in recognition, the teacher needs to provide assistance. The pupil must be asked to fill in with a meaningful word which makes sense in relationship to the other words in the sentence or even paragraph. Sometimes, the ridiculous is said and the learner must be aided in realizing that the word provided by the pupil does not make sense. If the pupil still is not able to provide the needed word, he/she needs to view the initial consonant of the unknown word. These initial consonants are quite consistent between symbol and sound. Additional phonic emphasis, as the need arises, may be stressed in assisting learners in word identification techniques.
- ***recognizing common syllables.*** There are consistently pronounced syllables in reading social studies content that will help pupils to become proficient readers. For example, pupils do study different nations in ongoing

lessons and units of study. Thus, the word "nation" crops up somewhat frequently. The syllable "tion" is consistently pronounced "shun." These consistencies in syllabic identification assist pupils in reading more fluently.

Comprehension of subject matter becomes the ultimate goal in reading. Careful reading is then salient. There are different level of comprehension. Pupils might identify selected facts frequently, but this represents the lowest level of comprehending subject matter being read. Understanding of facts in a broader context is necessary. Thus, the learner needs to relate these facts to a broader context. For instance, Jordan (a fact) is in the Middle East, but why is it important? This may be elaborated upon, among other things, with learning about refugees streaming in from the wars in Syria, as well as those from wars in Iraq. Going to a higher level in comprehension, pupils must analyze the causes of wars in this area of the Middle East. The crisis in neighboring Syria has a civil war going on between the followers of President Bashear Assaid versus the opposition rebels group. This alone has much attached history. There are numerous additional causes including disagreements among Shias, Alawites, and Sunnis. After analyzation, it is important to move forward with pupils developing major generalizations from subject matter acquired. Thus, conclusions must be stressed, otherwise a hodgepodge of isolated ideas might accrue. Thus, appraising the accuracy of content and its sources are important. Creativity is always to be encouraged with the identification of unique problems and innovative solutions.

Different levels of thinking may come about in collaborative settings whereby pupils share ideas in answering questions and solving problems. The class as a whole must have a supporting environment for pupils to contribute and accept other viewpoints. As soon as ridiculing of ideas occurs or as rudeness enters in, contributions from pupils go downhill in quality and amount.

Additional collaboration might well occur in small groups of four to five class members. In this setting, learners feel less restrained and might well contribute more freely. Ideas need to circulate within the group whereby all contribute and no one dominates the discussion. Staying on the topic being discussed is vital with high expectations from each participant. Then too, it is always poignant to meet needs of individual learners. A project method might work well here whereby the pupil with teacher supervision selects an activity in which purpose is involved. The plans for its fulfilment needs to relate to developing a high quality product. Doing the project involves appraising sequential work being ongoing as well as completed. The finished project then is also evaluated in terms of desired standards. These completed projects may be displayed for classmates as well as for pupils of other classrooms to observe (Ediger, 2009).

In Closing

There are selected questions which the social studies teacher must answer in developing lessons and units of study. These include:

- which objectives best help pupils in becoming a good citizen?
- which learning opportunities should be provided to achieve these objectives?
- which subject matter content from the social science disciplines as well as other academic disciplines need to be included?
- which evaluation techniques should be emphasized to ascertain learner achievement?

REFERENCES

Ediger, Marlow (2009), "Issues in the social studies," *Experiments in Education*, 37(4), 75-78.

Ediger, Marlow, and D. Bhaskara Rao (2012), *Essays on Teaching Social Studies*. New Delhi, India: Discovery Publishing House Pvt. Ltd.

33
Teaching New Social Studies

The new social studies has a vibrant emphasis with indepth teaching rather than survey procedures. Indepth teaching stresses the importance of pupils understanding concepts and generalizations more thoroughly than was true formerly. Rote learning and memorization are things of the past unless they are truly vital in ongoing lessons and units of study. Relevant generalizations which are understood and meaningful provide a framework for achieving ensuing objectives of instruction. These structural ideas make provisions for teaching subordinate content which support the major generalizations. Pupils perceiving the relationship of knowledge is poignant since better retention of previously encountered structural and subordinate subject matter is possible.

Indepth Teaching in the Curriculum

The social studies teacher needs to incorporate structural content in his/her daily/unit lesson planning. Carefully designed plans aid in focusing upon key subject matter, not trivia. The plans then provide a blue print for instruction and assists in achieving objectives of instruction. In my thirty school years of supervising university student teachers in the public schools, the writer noticed that those who planned well did a much better job of teaching pupils than those who planned haphazardly. It takes time to think through, critically and creatively, what needs to be taught, as well as realize that each day of instruction in the social studies is valuable. Using lesson/unit plans as guides to instruction also provides ample time for pupil input in identifying vital projects and raising salient questions (Ediger, 2011).

Cross-disciplinary procedures of instruction makes it possible to integrate vital concepts and generalizations across the different academic areas. Knowledge which is related has a better chance of pupil retention as compared to isolated facts. It also has opportunities to be utilized more so than content stressed in isolation. Relevancy emphasizes that practical use may be in the offing in identifying concepts and generalizations which possess utilitarian values. Frequency of use is then made of subject matter acquired.

A variety of learning opportunities must be in the offing which help learners to attain objectives. They need to provide for diverse styles of learning. Thus, selected pupils may prefer a hands on approach in learning whereas others might like abstractions, more so, such as those attained from reading/ writing experiences. A balance between the two is preferable since life itself requires both in everyday experiences. The following then, might well provide learning opportunities in the social studies:

- those involving concrete experiences such as excursions, antiques, objects and items, models, and student developed projects
- pictorial items including illustrations, paintings, drawings, time lines with related pictures, video-tapes, and slides
- abstract materials such as printed basal textbooks, graphs and charts, library books, technological and internet sources, and primary sources of information (Ediger and Rao, 2012).

Each of these sources used in teaching and learning situations builds upon the other in sequence as well as provide for indepth instruction. Then too, variety might well provide for different interests, and learning styles. Each pupil must have a social studies curriculum which benefits the self to achieve optimally. Social development needs to possess a significant part of teaching and learning. Thus, collaborative endeavors are poignant. Small groups should be arranged so that each pupil develops skills in working harmoniously with others. In the societal realm, individuals must be able to get along well with each other in school and in society. There are numerous times when collaborative activities may be implemented, as in small group problem-solving with an identified problem, hypothesis, data gathering from a variety of reference sources, and opportunities to appraise the hypothesis. Results must be shared with others in the classroom; communicating effectively is a shared goal and vital in any community. Attitudes to be developed here include, respecting others and their individual ideas, encourage each committee member to participate but not dominate committee endeavors, and ask questions if comments are not clear within the collaborative setting.

Reading primary and secondary sources are salient learning opportunities in the social studies. Here, pupils might need assistance in word identification techniques and these include:

- using syllabication, phonics, and syntax to recognize the unknown
- using picture clues, diagrams, and charts
- using context clues and semantics.

The use of context clues is probably the best procedure in the identification of unknown words. Thus, a learner needs to fill in with a word which fits in with the others in the sentence/paragraph. The supplied word must be meaningful and make sense in regard to the others. If this is not adequate, sounding out or using phonics with the first letter of the unknown word, generally, will aid. The rest of the above asterisked items might, also, be utilized as the need arises. Pupils tend to use a variety of approaches including the form/shape (configuration clues) of an unknown to assist in the identification process. The point being that the social studies teacher must have a wide repertoire of skills available to guide pupils in becoming effective, fluent readers.

There are numerous illustrations on printed pages to help pupils identify the correct word, from the unknown. This is especially true for primary age pupils. Then too, illustrations function to add meaning to a paragraph/selection being read. Pupils do need to learn to read pictures in order to comprehend subject matter. Pupils must learn to read across the curriculum which aids in practising the skill of reading to become self-efficacious in learning (Ediger, 2009).

Reading serves a variety of purposes. Reading to acquire vital facts is salient in that a specific kinds of information is necessary. However, higher levels of cognition must be emphasized such as critical reading whereby the accurate from the inaccurate is sorted as well as facts from opinions and the lesser valued from the more important information. Then too, pupils may read to generate creative thought such as in brainstorming for a conclusion. Reading for main ideas in separation from the subordinate also involves higher levels of cognition. Pupils need to learn to read for a variety of purposed in securing relevant information.

Evaluation of Pupil Progress

There are plethora of available evaluation techniques to appraise learner achievement. The social studies teacher must be a careful observer of each pupil to notice growth and progress. Thus, he/she may appraise the following, using teacher observation:

- analytical and critical thinking
- creativity and contributions made in class and in small groups
- quality of interactions in collaborative/small group work
- assisting in developing and maintaining a good learning environment
- improvement in fluent reading and comprehension
- use of technology in teaching and learning situations.

Additional tools to use in appraising learner progress include teacher written tests. In writing these test items, the teacher needs to be aware of validity and reliability concepts. The latter two concepts are indeed salient when standardized tests are selected and administered. The Manual of the standardized test provides necessary information on validity and reliability of the involved test. Ideally, results of/from the standardized test must be utilized along with other evaluation procedures to secure a total picture of the child's performance in the social studies. Thus, the following might also be utilized:

- rating scales and checklists
- rubrics.

Each evaluation result provides a check on the others and makes for a more compressive program of assessment.

REFERENCES

Ediger, Marlow (2009), "Issues in the Social Studies," *Experiments in Education*, 37(4), 75-78.

Ediger, Marlow (2011), "Oral Communication Across the Curriculum," *Journal of Instructional Psychology*, 38(3 and 4), 24-26.

Ediger, Marlow, and D. Bhaskara Rao (2012), *Essays on Teaching Social Studies*, New Delhi, India: Discovery Publishing House.

34

Teaching Social Studies

An Indepth Approach

Social studies has been neglected with it not be emphasized in NCLB testing in that what is tested is what will be taught. Being tested with NCLB tests also has its harmful effects due to factual items lending themselves to test taking. Multiple choice test items in NCLB make for rote learning and memorization in reports from different school systems whereby teachers may spend weeks drilling pupils on subject matter knowledge and the art of test taking. Better it is to emphasize higher levels of cognition in teaching and learning situations. Drilling pupils for taking a test does not make for enduring and thoughtful learning, but stresses regurgitation of subject matter which is of little possible use. Thus, unconnected bits of information are to accrue when pupils respond to multiple choice test items. Instead, social studies instruction must emphasize joy and excitement in learning. Pupils making discoveries and identifying problems and questions makes for a relevant social studies curriculum.Then too. learners need to make choices and decisions. Life consists of choosing from among alternatives (Ediger and Rao, 2012).

Developing the Social Studies Curriculum

Curriculum design in the social studies needs to be ongoing and continuous. Teachers and supervisors need to be on the lookout for ways of improvement in objectives, learning opportunities, and appraisal procedures. To live in a technological age requires that individuals be knowledgeable, interested, and perceive purpose in improving society. The author was born in 1927 when his family drove a Model A Ford with a starter when some used a hand crank to start the car. There were no heaters in these cars and the windshield wiper had to be operated by hand. They drove about 35 miles per hour and started to vibrate when driven a little bit faster. In 1937, my parents bought a 1937 Plymouth and what a joy it was to have a heater in the car. The windshield wiper was electrically operated and kept the windshield free from rain and defrosted the windows for better vision in winter. The maximum speed driven was, approximately, 45-50 miles per hour. The car battery "ran down" very quickly when starting the car on a cold day. Our grange, attached to the barn, had a little hill, making it possible to push it downhill to start the car with a mechanical gear shift.

Compare the above with new car models which:

- can readily go 85 miles per hour easily, readily defying speed limits.
- have air conditioning and excellent heaters as standard equipment; the engine starts even when temperature readings fall to/below 20 degrees Fahrenheit.
- ride very smoothly at almost any speed and all have good radios. Our 1937 Plymouth had no radio and very few cars did at that time.
- power steering, automatic drive, and power brakes, among other features.

So much for the above comparisons in automobiles. This says to us that the curriculum also must change in time. I- Pads are four to five years since their inception with many schools having adopted them for many classes. My high school of graduation, Inman, Kansas (city of eleven hundred people) purchased i-Pads for all students for the 2011-2012 school year, with many technological advances already in place.

With much knowledge available, pupils need guidance to focus on major ideas, not trivia nor irrelevant facts. This attempts to answer the question in broad outline, "What should be taught?" Key ideas provide structure in learning as well as a framework for pupils studying each structure, carefully defined and developed, with intensified teaching. Supporting subject matter give strength to each structural idea.

A variety of kinds of learning opportunities must be provided. Each activity reinforces those inherent ideas, making for indepth teaching. Careful and meticulous sequencing provides opportunities for success in pupil achievement. Ensuing subject matter acquired, based upon what was taught previously, directly relates the new with the old in concepts and generalizations taught. Then too, learning by discovery makes for excitement as well as interest in achievement. Instead of lecture, pupil involvement invites learner questions and problem identification. This does involve brain storming in a plethora of cases. With inquiry methods of instruction, pupil collaboration is needed whereby they:

- stay on the topic unless additional worthwhile problems are selected and identified
- respect and accept each other as human beings and not as objects
- contribute, individually, to the ongoing discussion to make for indepth learning
- summarize conclusions to use in new or novel situations
- do something with learnings acquired such as writing creative verse and poetry, making a classroom booklet of main ideas obtained, keeping diary and/or log entries
- do an art project, mural, frieze, among other visual arts, pertaining to indepth generalizations and concepts (Ediger, 2009).

Reading in the Social Studies

Pupils need to read primary sources. These are original in its entirety and written by a eye witness account. One of the writer's graduate students brought to class a diary with the actual dated accounts of a Civil War relative. The handwriting was clear on the aged yellow pages revealing the style used at that time. Some of the content, the diary writer wrote, was in an abbreviated form, but was generally decipherable. This was read aloud by the teacher as students followed along on the clearly legible screen. There was considerable excitement and interest in the diary contents. Several sessions were spent on its reading and discussion, along with other internet primary sources. Students learned how to integrate and relate primary sources with ongoing units of study.

Secondary sources are good to use, providing they are accurate and on the reading levels of involved learners. These secondary sources include carefully chosen basal textbooks, as well as information based library books. Different word recognition techniques need to be emphasized for those pupils needing assistance in identifying the unknown. These include context and picture clues, phonics, and syllabication. Content analysis is definitely salient in order to aid indepth comprehension. This includes:

- reading to secure vital facts
- reading to obtain poignant concepts and generalization
- reading for a sequence of ideas
- reading to appraise subject matter
- reading to compare/contrast sources of information
- reading to analyze and synthesize subject matter
- reading to perceive cause/effect relationships.

Subject matter secured must be discussed indepth involving critical and creative thought. Relevant subject matter and discussions provide a plethora of opportunities to utilize what has been learned. The total social studies curriculum must emphasize developing the good citizen and this needs to be stressed with poignant subject matter knowledge, model behaviour during classroom endeavors as well as in the school setting. Respect for others is always important!

Evaluation of Achievement

Diverse procedures need to be utilized in indepth unit instruction in the social studies. Teacher observation of pupil behaviour in ongoing lessons and units of study in terms of definite standards of conduct. Assessing pupil products in the classroom/school setting, directly related to a social studies unit, should be emphasized. A carefully developed rubric may be developed and used here. Teacher written tests help the teacher in formative and summative evaluation ascertain what has been mastered and what needs additional teaching and learning. Pupil self-evaluation, using a carefully devised score card, guides pupils in achieving more optimal progress. Additional appraisal procedures should include the following:

- standardized tests which measure social studies achievement in subject matter knowledge as well as in thinking skills and in attitudinal development
- diagnostic tests which assess where learners need more help in specifically.

All measurement devices need to be valid. Thus, standardized tests, for example to be valid, should measure salient achievement in social studies content and not in another academic discipline. It must not posses test items which contain highly complex words and thus become a test of reading abilities.

To be reliable, the test needs to measure consistency of pupil test results. Both validity and reliability data are provided in the Manual for the adopted test.

Conclusion

Relevant facts, concepts and generalizations must be chosen as objectives for pupil achievement. Aligned learning opportunities with a variety of activities stresses indepth teaching. Evaluation procedures should be varied and assist in ascertaining pupil progress.

REFERENCES

Ediger, Marlow (2009), "Issues in the Social Studies," *Experiments in Education*, 37(4), 75-78.

Ediger, Marlow, and D. Bhaskara Rao (2012), *Essays on Teaching Social Studies*. New Delhi, India: Discovery Publishing House Pvt. Ltd.

35

Teaching Social Studies Indepth

Social studies, too frequently, is taught in a survey approach whereby pupils obtain subject matter in a shallow manner. Forgetting and hazy recalls are typical of this procedure of instruction. Covering many topics in a relatively short period of time does not make for achievement which is long-lasting. Then too, selected pupils might be left behind in the hastening process. It takes time for content to soak in. Reflection, also, is necessary for pupils to make use of knowledge and skills when rehearsing what has been learned previously. Reflecting might emphasize the recollection of questions and problems over the previous lessons covered, resulting a more indepth procedure of instruction. Thus, learnings acquired lead in the direction of knowledge and skills being taught by using different methods, from deductive to inductive procedures, or utilization of concrete and semi-concrete materials of teaching (Ediger and Rao, 2012).

Updating the Social Studies

Basic needs must be fulfilled if learners are to achieve more optimally. This is essential for improved achievement in all curriculum areas. Thus, the following need to be sustained:

- adequate nutritious food, quality shelter, and appropriate clothing
- a safe environment
- feelings of love and belonging

- recognition for things well done or where improvement has taken place.

Each of the above asterisked items might also become salient as integrated subject matter/content in ongoing units of study.

Social studies has been omitted from state mandated tests and is essential for adequate attention in educating the total person. Thus, social studies teachers need to choose with great care vital objects for pupil achievement, fascinating related learning opportunities to attain the stated objectives, as well as valid/reliable appraisal procedures to ascertain growth and and progress. Thus, poignant structural ideas in any unit of study need to be chosen. These provide a framework or structure for pupils to perceive relevancy in subject matter and skills in ensuing lessons. Subordinate ideas acquired are then integrated with the structure as well as assisting in achieving relevant subject matter. Perceiving connectedness is important and provides for situations whereby content is increasingly enduring as well as being retained more effectively. Indepth teaching is involved here. Pupils then meet up with similar/same ideas, but presented in diverse ways. Subject matter is more usable in these teaching and learning situations and is not taught to be memorized, rather rich activities and experiences abound for meaning. It is not valuable solely for testing purposes but to be utilized in functional situations. Although doing well in test results is salient, broader uses must be made.

Learning experiences need to implement the psychology of instruction. There are selected criteria which social studies teachers need to follow:

- high expectations for learner attainment are being emphasized, but are achievable. Learnings which are too complex have a tendency for pupils to experience excessive failure.
- interest is a powerful factor in learning and makes for pupil effort in goal attainment. Boring activities have long been criticized by educators.

- purposeful experiences indicate that learners accept reasons for achieving. Too frequently, pupils do not perceive reasons for participation and thus minimal learning takes place.
- motivation for achieving must take place. Motivationless pupils are somewhat lethargic in attitudes toward objectives attainment within ongoing lessons (Ediger, 2013).

Activities and experiences need changing to meet challenging needs of pupils. There are a variety to develop and maintain pupil meaning. For instance, the writer watched a video on Life during the Middle Ages which portrayed interesting and accurate subject matter. Pupils then may observe:

- life on a manor with the nobleman's castle, the village church, and surrounding cottages for peasants. Peasants were out in the fields cutting wheat with a scythe on a hot summer day. Being self-sufficient is a key concept dealing with life on a manor
- guild members at work advancing through the ranks of apprentice, journeyman, and master
- becoming a knight - page, assistant, and knighthood
- members of a monastery in which individuals separated themselves from society and doing work involving the church.

With video-tapes such as that above, pupils tend to get the feel of living during the Middle Ages. During the presentation, pupils may think of questions and problems to solve relating to its contents. Indepth research for answers/ solutions might then be found. Ample time must be provided for elaborate discussion, followed by summaries and conclusions developed collaboratively. This might well lead to the utilization of primary sources in the ongoing unit of study. There are a plethora of writings available (such as internet sources and classical literature books) from the Middle Ages period of time. These should be on the understanding level of learners and may be read aloud and collectively to take care of problems in word recognition. Time and place of written work varies much in terms of sentence structure, word order and meaning, as well as words themselves. With proper introduction, many pupils find the use of primary sources to be interesting. With the use of an overhead projector, or electronic device, to enlarge the printed materials, each learner might well observe the contents clearly. To reiterate, the ensuing subject matter from the primary source may be read aloud and collectively with teacher guidance. Thus, word recognition difficulties might be minimized. Meaningful reading is poignant!

Any reading experience may be made more semi-concrete and concrete through the implementation of learning activities as in the following:

- making models such as a castle and cottages
- doing a creative dramatics activity of a scene from life on a manor
- creating an advertisement pertaining to a tournament to be held on the manor
- giving a class report on the Guilds of the Middle Ages
- engaging in making a mural on Monastic Life.

Each of the above asterisked items may be appraised in terms of:

- accuracy and being aesthetically pleasant
- neatness in its making and doing
- effort put forth
- cooperation among participants.

Other classrooms may be invited to see and observe the projects. Sharing with others what has been learned is salient and encourages innovation in the school setting. At the same time, indepth learning is being emphasized. Each facet of the Middle Ages is being stressed as learners participate actively in ongoing lessons within the unit of study (Ediger, 2011).

Evaluation of Pupil Progress

Teacher observation needs to be used continuously to notice achievement. In daily lessons, the social studies teacher might well take note of the following:

- the attention span of individual learners. Where it is short, inspiring learning opportunities need to be in evidence.
- diligence in handing in assignments on time. The teacher needs to provide meaningful subject matter, making for attainable results.
- work study habits whereby learners are wholehearted involved in an ongoing experience.
- resilience in which a pupil bounces back from experiencing frustration or defeat. Pupils need assistance to be successful since this builds upon future successes.
- reflection upon what has been acquired. With reflection, the learner utilizes feedback from previously achieved subject matter and skills to identify questions and fill loopholes in learning.
- critical thinking whereby pupils analyze subject matter into facts versus opinions, fantasy from reality, as well as accurate from inaccurate information.
- creative thought in which the learner comes up with unique, original ideas as in related art projects, poetry writing, as well as story telling and writing.

Standardized, valid and reliable, may also provide feedback pertaining to how well each pupil is achieving in the social studies. An items analysis gives information and needs to be studied by teachers to note which test items have been missed and appraise if the missed item should become an objective for teaching and learning situations. Learner achievement and progress needs to be monitored continuously. These items, if deemed relevant, should be integrated in an ongoing lesson/unit of study.

Emphasized missed items in drill sessions is not recommended unless they are considered vital. Otherwise salient knowledge and skills are remembered sooner if integrated. Standardized test results are usually recommended because they present an exact numeral in terms of learner progress such as a percentile/standard deviation. The numerical results make it easier to communicate with the lay public involving pupil progress as compared to direct teacher statements such as report cards and letters of attainment.

REFERENCES

Ediger, Marlow (2013), "Seven Criteria for an Effective Classroom", *Edutracks*, 12(11), 12-13.

Ediger, Marlow (2011), "Learning Stations in the Social Studies", *Education*, 131 (3), 467-470.

Ediger, Marlow, and D. Bhaskara Rao (2012), *Essays on Teaching Social Studies*. New Delhi, India: Discovery Publishing House Pvt. Ltd.

36

Teaching the Social Studies with a New Emphasis

Social studies instruction took a back seat when the No Child Left Behind (NCLB) law which was implemented in 2002. Reading and mathematics were the two key curriculum areas tested upon with science following in 2009. Teachers felt pressured to have pupils achieve well in order to be promoted in grades three through eight. Much time was then spent in classroom drill, thus omitting social studies the fine arts, and physical education.

With the Common Core State Standards (CCSS) coming into being, forty-six states have signed on to being a part whereby new objectives and measurement procedures for pupils will be in vogue. How will the new social studies be different?

Common Core and the Social Studies

Social studies units of instruction will emphasize more of indepth teaching and learning. Survey methods of the past stressed covering much ground in a relatively short period of time. This lead to shallowness in learner thinking whereby many facts might soon be forgotten. Indepth thought stresses the saliency of achieving vital concepts and generalizations with intensive thinking. Thus, for example to attach meaning to the concept of Crusader in a unit of study on the Middle Ages, pupils need to view illustrations, see a videotape, read about, draw, and make models of crusaders from clay. Many learnings then accrue intensifying to the concept of Crusader. A generalization shows relationships among concepts, and these too, need indepth study for their achievement. The generalization—Crusaders fought for control of the Holy Land—requires relating the previously studied concept, Crusaders, with the Holy Land. Indepth study of why an area is named the Holy Land is needed. The Holy Land needs accrued learnings from a world map which shows the routes Crusaders took from Europe to the land of Palestine. The walled city of Jerusalem contains the Church of the Holy Sepulcher. A video of this Church shows the identified Tomb of Christ and why this, among other places, was poignant to the Crusaders. Also, Bethlehem, six miles south, has the Church of the Nativity, the recognized birthplace of Christ. There are a plethora of travel brochures, computer information sources, and knowledgeable people who have travelled many times to the Holy Land and might well provide necessary subject matter for both churches. For indepth teaching to occur, a variety of rich activities need to be in the offing to shed indepth knowledge of salient concepts and generalizations (Ediger and Rao, 2013).

Second, meaning making must be inherent in each learning activity. Without meaning, ideas become hazy an vague. Better it is if each pupil attaches meaning to and in ongoing experiences. Each experience listed above then needs to have related discussions pertaining to the content. In these discussions pupils may ask questions and make vital comments relating directly to each specific scenes. Raising questions of what is not understood, as well as what more is desired in learning about the Crusaders and the Crusades may be covered indepth in the discussions. Critical thinking is involved if pupils seek to determine accurate from inaccurate information. Discussions are relevant ways of learning intensively if pupils stay on the topic, all members are involved, and respect for ideas accrue (Ediger, 2011).

Third, wholehearted involvement is necessary for pupils to feel engaged in the ongoing lesson and unit of study. There must be many items of interest for each learner to do and achieve. Pupils, individually, need to feel accepted and possess feelings of belonging. In observing my university student teachers (ST) in the public school setting, one ST together with the cooperating teacher worked with pupils in developing a mural on the Holy Land, by placing cities therein such as Hebron, Caesarea, Bethany, Jericho, as well as the Sea of Galilee and the Horns of Hattin. The Horns of Hattin is located five miles west of the Sea of Galilee and is the place where the Crusaders surrendered to Saladin, the Muslim General in 1187, ending the first Crusade which began in AD 1099. Here, pupils might learn about basic beliefs of Muslims such as saying the Creed for believers, facing Mecca in Saudi Arabia (birthplace of Mohammed the final prophet of Islam) five times each day when praying, making a minimum of one pilgrimage to Mecca during one's life time, and giving alms to the poor. The Crusades emphasized capturing the Holy Land from Moslems (Ediger and Rao, 2007).

Fourth, purpose for learning is salient in each lesson and unit of study. Learners then accept reasons for achieving objectives of instruction. Social studies should assist pupils, individually, in becoming good citizens in society. Knowledgeable as well as skilful citizens possess a solid background of information on their own nation and have abilities in getting along well with others in society. A quality current events program in the social studies guides learners to perceive the relevance of what is being studied of the past and its relationship to the present. Thus in current events, the following will be recurring happenings in the Holy Land:

- the Gaza Strip is made up of people who are refugees/ descendants of refugees from the land of Palestine, in 1948
- Israel became a nation in 1948 and has become very powerful militarily with a modern air force, navy, and army
- Syria with its vicious civil war. Syria lost the Golan Heights in the six day war of 1967 to Israel
- Egypt was the only Arab nation to sign a peace treaty with Israel in 1979 and received in return the Sinai

Peninsula which was captured by Israel in the 1967 six day war

- Jordan lost the West Bank to Israel in the 1967 six-day war. The Walled city of Jerusalem has inside its walls the Church of the Holy Sepulcher. The beautiful octagonal (moslem) Dome of the Rock built in AD 491, and the Western Wall which is the only remnant of the ancient Jewish temple. The walled city was annexed by Israel in 1967 and has changed from a Moslem population to one made up largely of Jews.
- Holy sites are very important to both Arabs and Jews presently. Both want the land of Palestine. This causes conflicts in the Holy Land. The writer was a teacher and relief worker on the West Bank with the Mennonite Central Committee, 1952-54 and has made five return trips. Israel with its modern military has been able to maintain occupation of captured lands. An Israel/Gaza war completed in eight days, November 2012. resulted in a draw, but heavy loses occurred in Gaza in particular and also in Israel with rockets hitting southern Israel as well as a few in Tel Aviv and in the rural Jerusalem area.

Fifth, the reading and writing connection is poignant. For many of the above-named happenings in history, much research and writing might accrue. A variety of reading sources may be used as references including basal textbooks, information based library books, encyclopaedias, and the internet. The writer when serving as a teacher in the early 1950s in Friends Boys School in Ramallah, Jordan (now the Occupied West Bank) read the Beirut, Lebanon Daily Star in the teacher's lounge regularly. He now reads this newspaper daily on the internet as well as the Jerusalem Post. What has been read may also be summarized in written work. Additional writing experiences to emphasize in the reading/writing connection include:

- writing play parts of a selected incident for a formal dramatization activity

- developing a bulletin board display with student writing below each illustration
- doing a social studies section in a portfolio pertaining to each pupil's written and related art products in ongoing units of study
- keeping a diary on achievements for each day of the week on social studies learnings
- summarizing diary entries into a log, much reading and writing accrues in this activity.

The social studies teacher, always, must be on the lookout for creative experiences in pupils making the reading/writing connection.

Sixth, developmentally appropriate primary sources, as distinguished from secondary sources, should be experienced by learners. Primary sources need emphasis in teaching and learning situations since they are eye witness accounts of actual happenings. Sometimes, an old diary is found in the attic of a person which dates back to recorded entrees, for example, during the Civil War (1861-1865). This diary has accounts written by a civil war soldier. These primary sources differ from secondary sources in that the latter who wrote about the civil war did not encounter these scenes, but wrote about what someone else had written. Most materials used in teaching history and the social studies are secondary in nature since eye witness accounts are lacking. When the writer in his early experiences (early/middle 1960s) in supervising student teachers observed a resource person, a former worker in the Civilian Conservation Corps (CCC) in the middle 1930s tell of his experiences. During the Great Depression of the 1930s, young men who joined the CCC found employment by building artificial lakes and dams, school and civic buildings, parks, as well as roads. These were governmental funded projects. Pictures were shown with classroom pupils being highly interested in this activity. Very few, if any, are living today of those who worked in the CCC.

Seventh, subject matter in the social studies needs to be integrated with other academic disciplines, where feasible.

This should enrich content for learners and not done for the sake of its doing. Thus, social studies lessons and units of study needs to aid pupils to experience rich learning activities which assist learners to experience wholeness in the integrated curriculum. However, the focal point is history and the social studies. Thus in a unit of study on the Middle East, pupils, for instance, might study the following in an integrated curriculum:

- art work design and products of Arabic and Jewish cultures
- music of native people in the Holy Land
- languages used in communication, orally and in written work
- historic buildings and architectural structures, as well as archeological sites for discovering ancient places and artifacts
- games played by children as well as athletic events in the Middle East.

Conclusion

Pupils need to attain relevant, salient objectives of instruction. They must stress knowledge as well as attitudinal goals. Diverse learning opportunities need to be provided so that each pupil can be successful in achievement. Valid and reliable procedures must be utilized to ascertain if objectives have been attained.

REFERENCES

Ediger, Marlow (2011), "Learning Stations in the Social Studies," *Education*, 131(3),467-470.

Ediger, Marlow, and D. Bhaskara Rao (2007), *Teaching Social Studies*, New Delhi, India: Discovery Publishing House Pvt. Ltd.

Ediger, Marlow, and D. Bhaskara Rao (2013), *Curriculum and School Teacher*, New Delhi, India: Discovery Publishing House Pvt. Ltd.

37

Reading in Social Studies

Although there are a plethora of additional rich learning activities, pupils do much reading in the social studies. Social studies teachers then need to be teachers of reading. Thus, a thorough knowledge of unit content is necessary along with skills in the methodology of instruction. Instruction must be adapted to the level of optimal understanding of learners. To challenge pupils, scaffolding needs emphasis to stress higher levels of attainment. The scaffold must be such that it increases achievement, but not for the sake of doing so nor to frustrate the learner. Pupil motivation is salient in teaching and learning situations and needs prime consideration in ongoing lessons and units of study (Ediger, 2013).

Social Studies in Ensuing Lessons

There are many facts which might be taught, making isolated learnings possible. Instead, the teacher needs to select carefully the broad or structural ideas within a unit. These ideas might well become main concepts and generalizations of unit teaching. Inductively, pupils with teacher leadership and inquiry methods may attain relevant content rather than isolated facts. From unit teaching, pupils might well attain subordinate subject matter which supports the broader or main idea. The teacher needs to be skilled in emphasizing probing in teaching and learning situations. Here, learners have identified vital questions and problems with involved efforts in ascertaining solutions. At this point, the text being read may be utilized in locating needed information.

Information obtained might well be verified from these abstract materials. The verification principle is salient in reading subject matter in order to secure more accurate information as well as checking comprehension through rereading. Indepth reading in searching for information is being emphasized. This is somewhat opposite of survey approaches where skimming for information results. This is a more shallow comprehension procedure as compared to indepth reading of subject matter.

Information sources, other than the text, might come from additional reputable reading materials. Pupils need to learn to read diverse illustrations, related to the ongoing activity. These include the following:

- reading illustrations in context. These may provide much accurate information when seeing pictures pertaining to the abstract.
- reading graphs such as line, bar, picture, and pie graphs.
- reading charts including narrative, flow, sequence, and illustration charts which provide valuable information.
- reading time lines pertaining to biographies, sequence of events, and salient happenings.
- side bars provides necessary info to assist pupils attaching meaning to ensuing context.

Too frequently, the sentences, paragraphs, and pages of text materials, alone, are perceived worthy of concentration by the pupil; however, illustrations, graphs, and charts add enrichment and understanding of subject mater read. Words in bold print or underlined should also receive much attention during the act of reading subject matter.

Vocabulary development is vital in social studies lessons and units of study. The vocabulary load might be heavy in selected pages and need pupil indepth understanding. New words might appear in print on the whiteboard or chalkboard. Ensuing words are then carefully noticed for each and pronounced acceptedly. They need either defining/used in meaningful sentences so that learners recognize each when reading the text. New words may appear in print on a word wall for pupil reference. It is interesting to note how frequently pupils will use the words on the word wall in reading subject matter since they have been viewed during a pupil's spare time. Additional procedures in word recognition and meaning include the following:

- putting in a word for the unidentified by furnishing one which makes sense. This also aids in vocabulary development.
- looking at an illustration contained in the text which might provide the correct word. This works well for young pupils, in particular, where picture clues are heavy. Then too, meanings are provided for vocabulary terms by looking at the illustrations.
- looking in the glossary for contextual terms in the basal textbook. This takes time to do so which hinders comprehension, in degrees.

Electronic texts might well offer a solution here.

- having a designated person pronounce the unidentified to the learner so that the learner experiences sequence in reading.

Pupils need to reflect upon subject matter read. This is a metacognitive strategy which assists in reviewing, rehearsing, and identification of unanswered questions and solutions to problems. Pupils forget less and the repertoire for recalling tends to increase. Social studies teachers must model how reflection generally operates. It invites inquisitiveness when learners perceive gaps in their very own knowledge and skills. This leads to searching for new information and content which invites learner growth in the social studies. Using a variety of references sources including the internet helps to satisfy pupil curiosity in the reflexion process. When supervising university student teachers in the public schools, the writer observed a cooperating teacher provide an excellent model for reflective thinking which encouraged pupils to follow the demonstrated model. The next school day, the student teacher and the cooperating teacher asked pupils if they had done reflective thinking with the details being discussed in class by three pupils who were motivated to tell of their experiences. Building upon these experiences, further assistance in reflective thinking was emphasized. Pupils tend to have somewhat fleeting concentrations, but they seemingly developed reflecting thinking skills in these area. Time did not permit to view further extensions and growth of metacognition in this case due to the end of the semester (Ediger, 2012).

Conclusion

Pupils need to be able to compare and contrast text material in developing summaries as well as conclusions. Abstract materials in reading are clarified with the utilization of audio-visual materials which include video-tapes, related illustrations from the teacher's file, and slides, among other semi-concrete and concrete materials of instruction.

REFERENCES

Ediger, Marlow (2013), "The Teacher and Students in the Social Studies," *College Student Journal*, 47(4), 649-652.

Ediger, Marlow (2012), "Literature in the Social Studies": The Pupil, and the Teacher," *Journal of Instructional Psychology*, 39 (2), 80-82.

38

Issues in Testing and Measurement

There are a plethora of issues involved in the testing and measurement movement. There is a call for more creative endeavors for pupils as compared to measuring achievement. Creativity tends to generate ideas which might well be unique and novel as compared to testing which requires a correct answer as measured by electronic procedures. There is a dichotomy here in what is desired from teachers and learners. Might the two procedures be harmonized, or are there two independent philosophies involved in determining pupil achievement and progress?

Testing and Creativity

Testing with the use of multiple choice test items emphasizes precision in ascertaining exactness. There is one correct response in a multiple choice test item. With four distractors, one is the right response. This is based on Stimulus/Response psychology. For example, the stem of the multiple choice test item is the Stimulus, the Response being one of the four listed responses. The philosophy involved here emphasizes the thinking of E.L Thorndike when in the 1920s stated that whatever exists, exists in some amount, and if it exists in some amount, it can be measured. Knowledge, then, is objective, independent of the observer, and can be measured in its exactness.

Subjectivity occurs in determining multiple choice test items with the following involved factors:

- human beings choose and write these items; other persons/items could have been chosen instead.
- if aligned with Common Core Standards or No Child Left Behind, subjectivity is inherent in terms of which criteria should serve for the alignment.
- the wording of a test item brings in the human dimension, even though it is tested for clarity, along with others, in pilot studies.

Stimulus/Response psychology does not stress essay tests due to subjective scoring, in particular. A rubric might be developed and used in the scoring process to make for more objectivity in scoring, but this might leave for much leeway of interpretation of pupil's answers. Multiple choice tests have a single correct answer and a single key is used in mass machine scoring. These tests emphasize the concept of closure in that a pupil is limited to correct, objective responses only. To write multiple choice test items, the writer generally needs to concentrate upon a stem with four possible responses, one of which is correct. It is difficult to think about four plausible responses. So often, one or two might be ridiculous. If one is a bad response, then it is a multiple choice test item with three possibilities in responding. If two sound partly or wholly irrational, it becomes a true false test. When teaching a university graduate Language Arts course, the writer had ninety-two students in a five-week summer session. He believes in measuring student achievement when using a mixed approach of test items, including essay test items. The perception was that to evaluate two separate interval administered essay tests was not reasonable within the five weeks. The writer then switched to the use of multiple choice test items only; these could be machine scored in a matter of minutes! Much time was spent in writing a 100 item multiple choice test, discovering, too, that a single comma is necessary in a test item to make for clarification.

We read much about teachers getting pupils in the public schools ready for taking mandated standardized tests, involving heavy use of drill and rote learning. Evidently, some public schools spend hours and hours of time here. Is there a better means of educating young people in the public school setting? Using the principles of psychology, the following guidelines are salient in choosing learning experiences:

- securing the interests of learners is poignant.
- assisting pupils to attach meaning within ongoing experiences.
- helping each pupil perceive purpose or reasons for achieving in place of forced drill.
- guiding learners to experience sequence in ongoing activities instead of isolated drill.

Instead of zeroing in within ongoing objectives of instruction, pupils should have ample opportunities to ask questions and seek answers. This might well mean broadening the horizons of pupils to develop indepth leanings. Curiosity in learning is fundamental in achieving more optimally as well as continually growing in knowledge and skills. Then too, problem solving stresses pupil interest and meaning. These are vital problems and spark the desire of pupils to develop hypotheses, test each hypothesis, and draw possible conclusions. Best it is, if these identified problems come from learners, and a variety of references sources are utilized to attain and test hypotheses. When questions and problems come from pupils, there can, indeed, be much enthusiasm for learning.

This does not minimize a more formal teaching and learning situation with its rather closely knit scope and sequence. These may be integrated into the total curriculum as well as can less formal discussions.

Discussions, in large group and small committees might well be evaluated in terms of up to date criteria, such as the following:

- all need to participate with no one dominating
- participants need to stay on the topic unless purpose is involved in integrating related subject matter from other academic disciplines

- clarity in content presented is vital
- identification of problems and questions are to be welcomed
- indepth treatment of ideas is to be emphasized (Ediger, 2011).

Multiple Choice Test Items

Too frequently, multiple choice test items are written very factually and can ultimately be memorized for testing purposes. Rather, these kinds of test items need to emphasize higher levels of cognition. To be sure, one needs to recall information prior to doing critical and creative thinking. But the recall level is the beginning of cognitive processes. Life in society demands higher levels of cognition to problem solve. Selected problems are very complicated in arriving at solutions and might well take years to obtain necessary solutions. Thus, when readiness is in evidence, pupils need to engage in problem solving experiences. Continual attempts must be made in developing multiple choice test items which measure critical and creative thinking. This is difficult to do since the emphasis is upon closure when a correct response is chosen form among four distractors.

Essay tests may be written with more open-ended approaches. Pupils, too, might do more interpreting in terms of responses made. This is not anarchy, but stresses the saliency of branching out to new ensuing ideas, directly related to the stated question. Recall of facts might well be a part of responses made. To reiterate, facts do support main ideas to provide structural content. Essay tests may do the following:

- emphasize pupil understanding of subject matter whereby he/she indicates comprehension.
- stresses pupil sequencing of ideas presented, not presented in isolated fashion.
- indicates that pupils can apply knowledge and skills.
- implies that critical and creative thinking abound.

- pupil use of grammar appropriately.
- perceiving the relationship of knowledge.

In essay testing, the evaluator need to be aware of pupils doing a large amount of writing for the sake of doing so, without stating salient ideas. Creative ideas are poignant if they relate to the topic expressed. Thus, unique, novel content is invited and presented in an original way. Critical thinking is wanted in the separation of facts from opinions, fantasy from reality, as well as accurate from inaccurate information. Clarity of expression is needed in essay test responses. Salient facets in grammar are necessary in the written content. A well developed rubric may assist in evaluating essay test items. It is important for the teacher to appraise separately test item #one for all pupils doing the test and then appraising item two for all pupils, followed by number three and so on in order to focus upon upon consistency for appraising each response for all pupils before going on to number two and so on. Weight may be given to a test item response as being more important than others, depending upon perceived worth.

Appraising Teachers Based on Pupil Standardized Test Results

There is much debate upon how teachers should be evaluated. Usually, standardized test results of pupils enter into the equation. Mandated test results, in particular, are strongly recommended by some or many educators as well as test publishers. Thus, multiple choice test results are favored.

There are a plethora of pieces of the puzzle which enter into how well pupils do on these tests. A good teacher is highly salient, here. But, how much of teacher effectiveness is involved when drill is heavily used to prepare pupils for mandated testing purposes? It is a question which needs much discussion and debate. Then too, what about the following factors entering into how well pupils do on these tests?

- recognized abilities and talents possessed. Recent research indicates that the brain is somewhat plastic and subject to modification with rich environmental experiences.

- growing up in a socio-economic area which is safe from all violence and crime, have adequate income, prize learning in academic areas, travel to interesting places, sight see, orally communicate frequently with parents as well as others, possess computers and advanced technology.
- being emotionally valued as a family member and being involved in cultural activities such as playing a musical instrument, among others.
- having personal needs met such as nutritional meals as well as appropriate clothing.
- having feelings of belonging in the neighbourhood, including trustworthy friends.

From the above asterisked items, one can see how well pupils do in school possessing these amenities as compared to those who lack most or all of the above. The child in the total environment must be considered in school achievement and progress, and not solely the teacher in the school setting.

In closing

There are a plethora of tests which have been published and attempt to measure learner achievement and progress. The writers have the following involved concerns here:

- are these tests piloted adequately to take out weaknesses?
- have these tests been carefully validated to indicate validity factors?
- how reliable is each test and how was this established?

REFERENCES

Ediger, Marlow (2011), "Collaboration Versus Individual Endeavors in the Classroom," *Education*, 132 (1), 217-220.

Ediger, Marlow, (2007), "Seven Criteria for an Effective Classroom Environment," *College Student Journal*, 41 (4), 1370-1373.

Index